Rape in Period Drama Television

Rape in Period Drama Television

Consent, Myth, and Fantasy

Katherine Byrne and Julie Anne Taddeo

LEXINGTON BOOKS
Lanham • Boulder • New York • London

Published by Lexington Books
An imprint of The Rowman & Littlefield Publishing Group, Inc.
4501 Forbes Boulevard, Suite 200, Lanham, Maryland 20706
www.rowman.com

6 Tinworth Street, London SE11 5AL, United Kingdom

Copyright © 2022 The Rowman & Littlefield Publishing Group, Inc.

All rights reserved. No part of this book may be reproduced in any form or by any electronic or mechanical means, including information storage and retrieval systems, without written permission from the publisher, except by a reviewer who may quote passages in a review.

British Library Cataloguing in Publication Information Available

Library of Congress Cataloging-in-Publication Data

Names: Byrne, Katherine, 1978- author. | Taddeo, Julie Anne, author.
Title: Rape in period drama television : consent, myth, and fantasy / Katherine Byrne and Julie Taddeo.
Description: Lanham : Lexington Books, 2022. | Includes bibliographical references and index. | Summary: "Rape in Period Drama Television considers the representation of rape and rape myths as well as the audience response to it in a range of the most influential television period dramas of recent years"—Provided by publisher.
Identifiers: LCCN 2021056730 (print) | LCCN 2021056731 (ebook) | ISBN 9781793625854 (cloth) | ISBN 9781793625878 (paperback) | ISBN 9781793625861 (ebook)
Subjects: LCSH: Rape on television. | Masculinity on television. | Historical television programs—History and criticism.
Classification: LCC PN1992.8.R26 B97 2022 (print) | LCC PN1992.8.R26 (ebook) | DDC 791.45/6556—dc23/eng/20211118
LC record available at https://lccn.loc.gov/2021056730
LC ebook record available at https://lccn.loc.gov/2021056731

Dedication
We dedicate this book to all the victims and survivors of sexual violence, past and present. We also dedicate this book to our daughters in the hope that the future will be better for them to grow up in.

Contents

Acknowledgments		ix
Introduction		1
1	Rape Fantasy and the "Lawless" Eighteenth Century: *Poldark* and *Banished*	7
2	Rape Responses, Romance, and Rape-Revenge	23
3	"Dismissed, Ignored, and Woefully Underreported": Male Rape in *Bridgerton* and *Outlander*	43
4	Rape as a Weapon of War: *Das Boot* and *A Place to Call Home*	59
5	Procurement and Period Drama: Rape for Money in *Harlots*	77
6	"If You Can't Rape Your Wife, Who Can You Rape?": Marital Rape in *The Forsyte Saga* and *Poldark*	91
7	Rape and the Older Woman	107
Conclusion		123
Bibliography		127
Index		141
About the Authors		143

Acknowledgments

This book grew out of an article on rape in eighteenth-century themed period drama that we first published in 2019 for *Critical Studies in Television* (*CST*). Elke Weissmann and the anonymous peer reviewers for *CST* helped us sharpen our analysis for that article, some of which is reproduced in the first chapter of this book. It was that article that led to a fortuitous meeting at the annual conference of the Popular Culture Association/American Culture Association with Lexington Book's Cultural Studies editor, Judith Lakamper, who encouraged us to develop the article into a book-length project. She and the team at Lexington steered us through publication as we coped with the additional demands at home and at work due to the COVID-19 pandemic. We owe further thanks to Dr. Frank Ferguson, Dr. Giuliana Monteverde, and the COVID Recovery Fund for their support, and all the students and friends who helped us through conversations about rape and television, especially Nicole Hamilton and Jorden Dobbs McMenamin. Lastly, we are always grateful to our families who patiently support our television viewing because they know it is for a good cause.

Introduction

Period drama is one of the most popular television genres. To millions of viewers worldwide, it offers an accessible, entertaining way of learning about our shared histories. Still associated with "cozy" Sunday-night viewing, it is considered an escapist, romantic genre, which perhaps caters more than any other to the female gaze. However, from the most unapologetically glossy and sanitized portrayal of the past on our screens to the most gritty, rape is the pervasive plotline they nearly all share. This book will consider the representation, uses, and meanings of this crime, and the audience response to it, via analysis of several of the most influential period dramas of recent years. In doing so, it will uncover the unique and complex relationship this type of television has with rape.

As we will explore, sexual violence is often used to give authenticity and realism to shows, and, disturbingly, as a sensationalist means of chasing ratings. Some representations of the crime on our screens are even what we would call "lazy rapes," as we see in the opening episode of *Jamestown* (2017–): a rape occurs at the twelve-minute mark to denote the general lack of female power in the new settler colony while not addressing the act's psychological or physical impact on the victim herself. Rape, like the corset, has become almost a shorthand in period dramas for women's oppression in the past. Problematic as this may be, however, including these kinds of crimes does put rape "back into history" and provide a needed reminder that the past was in fact a very dangerous place for women (and some men). From a theoretical perspective, then, rape functions as a kind of "anti-heritage" device: a reaction against the nostalgia usually associated with period television. It also, of course, forms a comment on and about our own present, in which awareness of the prevalence of sexual abuse has increased in the wake of the #MeToo and #TimesUp movements, but in which legal and political processes have not yet caught up (Khomami 2017).

The shows we examine here are in dialogue with rape and its meanings both past and present. In most cases, there were almost immediate changes in the way the crime was screened after women began to unify behind the hashtag #MeToo in October 2017, refusing to continue to be silent about the sexual violence so many of them had endured. Those shows which had previously used rape as a too-common plot device, like *Outlander* (2014–), and shown it in graphic detail now began to turn the camera away from the act itself. Brianna's off-screen rape in season 4 of *Outlander* is hence much less gratuitous than the many previous rapes in the show, for example. Similarly, *Poldark* (2015–2019) moves from having an eroticized "ravishment" in 2016 to a brutal, completely unromanticized marital rape plot after #MeToo (even if, as we argue in chapter 6, the show still feels the need to defend its earlier story line, and its hero). In particular, an emphasis on the complicit bystanders and witnesses of rape in many of these shows is indicative of a new awareness that society as a whole is responsible for such crimes as Harvey Weinstein's and Jeffrey Epstein's.

Most of the period dramas we discuss here are British: *Downton Abbey* (2010-2015), *Poldark*, and other shows made in the UK still represent some of the most famous examples of the genre and are watched around the world. As a result, they represent the most widely disseminated and most debated rape representations on television. Britain is, of course, not the only country whose period dramas deal with sexual violence, however, and hence we also include some dramas from Germany, Australia, the United States, and Italy. Similarly, in the interests of coverage we have tried to cover or at least mention most of the period drama rape plotlines out there: the sheer amount of rape on our screens, however, means this is not entirely possible. We have structured our chapters by "types" of rape, or demographic of victim, in order to examine the different assumptions, myths, and representations that surround differing contexts for sexual violence in these shows. In doing so we do not, however, wish to suggest any support for the legal and social distinctions that for too long sought to distinguish "real rape" (violent stranger rape) from other "lesser" types of sexual violence (like acquaintance or marital rape). As we discuss throughout the book, all rape is equally abhorrent: thankfully, many (though not all) of the shows we examine share this view.

SCOPE OF THE BOOK

One of the most surprising aspects of period drama plots about rape is the romantic, erotic way it is frequently represented onscreen, and the enthusiastic response of fans who buy into these representations. The first chapter explores the continuing popular appeal of plotlines featuring "ravishment" in dramas set in the eighteenth century, a period itself that witnessed the birth of the romance novel and included scenarios much like the pressured, coercive seduction of female characters by period drama heroes like Ross Poldark. As Katie Roiphe argues, "In the realm of private fantasy, the allure of sexual submission, even in its extremes, is remarkably widespread" (2012). Roiphe is herself a polarizing writer, but these dramas reveal the extent to which that is still true and also that historical fictions provide the main means through which fans can explore such politically problematic fantasy.

In series like *Poldark* viewers are typically expected to excuse, even forgive, the actions of the handsome heroes, yet even when TV series attempt to focus on the female victim, her trauma often becomes secondary to the narrative action that follows her rape. Chapter 2 therefore examines how other characters in these shows respond to rape plotlines in their midst. Lisa M. Cuklanz, writing of late twentieth-century television, argued that rape plots were more interested in the male partners of the victims than those victims themselves (1999). Most of the dramas explored in chapter 2 reveal that very little has changed: period drama still focuses its rape narratives on its impact on masculinity and male identity. On the big screen the most popular rape narrative is the rape/revenge film in which (frequently) the female victim punishes her attacker: period drama, however, still seems more interested in revenge perpetuated by men defending a perceived slight on their masculinity. Rape plots in *Downton Abbey*, *A Place to Call Home* (APTCH 2013–2018), and *Outlander* demonstrate how rape is used to explore masculinity in our culture, and how the victim is reduced to a conduit for relationships between men.

Outlander, a show so preoccupied with rape that it has been dubbed "Rapelander" by fans on social media, merits even further attention in our third chapter as it is unique among television dramas in its repeated portrayal of male rape by men. Jamie's rape by Black Jack Randall at the end of season 1 was described as "the most disturbing rape on TV" (ignoring the multiple attempted and actual rapes of his wife Claire), and Randall also rapes Jamie's young ward, Fergus, while later, Jamie's nephew, Young Ian, is raped by a female character, the witch Geillis. Here we explore the multiple ways in which these rapes are used to address male trauma, emasculation, and shame. While these uses suggest that male trauma is still prioritized in period drama TV, season 4 of *Outlander* presents, as discussed in the previous chapter, in contrast, a story arc involving the rape of Brianna—notably, and unusually for the show, off screen. This, we argue, is one of the first examples of television responding positively to #MeToo while still promoting a male revenge scenario in its aftermath. In this chapter we also examine the recent hit Netflix show, *Bridgerton* (2020–), and the rape of its male lead by a woman. Not only was this nonconsensual act not taken seriously by the plot, it was also not recognized as rape by many fans, displaying how problematic assumptions about what the crime "looks like" still endure—even post-#MeToo.

Outlander frequently shows men at war, as Jamie takes part in the Scottish rebellion against the British in its first two seasons, and by the fifth season is preparing for war against the British in his new home in the colony of North Carolina. It is only in very recent years that the full horrors of war for women are beginning to be heard. In keeping with this, period dramas about war usually tend to focus on the damaged bodies or minds of the men who fought in the conflict. Chapter 4 examines recent shows set in, or shortly after, World War II, *Das Boot* (2018–) and *APTCH*, that stand out in how they use rape plots as a means to shift emphasis and narrative focus to the sometimes overlooked suffering of civilians and bystanders. A reworking of the classic 1981 German film and 1985 miniseries, *Das Boot* displays a feminist undertaking to represent female war trauma in parallel to that experienced by the male characters on the titular submarine. It also reflects a real shift in the unerotic representation of rape in keeping with its post-#MeToo production date. At the same time, *Das Boot* uses rape as a metaphor for the contested states that are being fought over and uses the violated female body as a signifier of conflicted land and nation. In *APTCH*, the lead character, Sarah Adams, has flashbacks to her years in a German concentration camp, where she, as a Resistance fighter and convert to Judaism, is spared death in exchange for "servicing" German SS officers. But her fiancé George Bligh, and even Sarah herself, must come to terms with her experiences as *rape*, thus underscoring how the act of survival further disrupts any notion of consent. *APTCH* is anxious to separate Australian national identity from war rape, however, constructing it as a crime committed, alongside many others, solely by the Nazis. History has shown, however, that all sides in war took the opportunity to inflict sexual violence, and that conflict can make any man a rapist. This chapter explores the Allied investment in "othering" war rape and how *Das Boot* is one of the few shows to acknowledge that this crime is much closer to home.

All acts of rape are about power, and recent events in the media show the extent to which institutionalized sexual abuse has long been big business. The fall of comedian and actor Bill Cosby revealed the corruption and cover-up at the heart of show business, for example, and the Weinstein and Epstein papers/trials have further revealed the ways in which procurement, money, and power have intersected. Perhaps because it is still often a conservative medium, mainstream period drama tends to shy away from critiquing capitalism, though, and in this regard *Harlots* (2017–) is highly unusual in its subject matter: as a result we think it merits its own chapter. This critically acclaimed, female-dominated show follows the fortunes of a group of sex workers in Georgian London, with plotlines which examine the motivations of men and women who benefit financially from sexual crime, and the institutional and pervasive nature of rape for money. In its representation of city life for lower-class women it is the very antithesis of *Bridgerton*, and particularly in its much more serious handling of rape. Sexual violence in the eighteenth-century setting of the show is sanctioned by the state, and either ignored or facilitated by its apparatuses of power. *Harlots* hints that things may not have changed greatly. Of course, TV's representation of rape as business is complicated by its own exploitation of the crime for ratings, however, and *Harlots* displays an awareness of this problematic culpability.

We mention earlier that rape plotlines are one of the few instances where period drama is not unapologetically nostalgic. The grittiness of violence and unromanticized prostitution in *Harlots* is a good example of this, but perhaps nothing makes the viewer deeply thankful to live in modern and more enlightened times than plots featuring marital rape. In chapter 6 we discuss the film *The Duchess* (2008) and the TV series *The Forsyte Saga* and *Poldark*, both their twentieth- and twenty-first-century adaptations, which feature marital rape adapted from their original source texts (the novels of John Galsworthy and Winston Graham, respectively). But the two represent a stark contrast in response to the rapes shaped by viewers' attraction (or lack thereof) to the rapist in each series. In *The Forsyte Saga*, the male lead in both the 1967 and 2002 versions had already established their heartthrob status, and this is part of the reason why audience responses to this rape were so unsympathetic toward the survivor. Both adaptations reveal how marital rape was still, in the twentieth and twenty-first centuries, judged differently from other types of sexual violence. Winston Graham, however, fashioned *Poldark*'s marital rapist, the Reverend Osborne "Ossie" Whitworth, as a gluttonous sadist who repeatedly rapes his young wife, Morwenna, rather than a one-off act like Soames's rape of Irene Forsyte. Ossie's character is also set up as a foil to Ross Poldark so that the viewer can forgive one act of rape (*Poldark*'s "bedroom encounter" discussed in our first chapter) but not the repeated brutality of the other. Season 5 of *Poldark*, which aired in 2019, is not based on Graham's novels but original material written by Debbie Horsfield, and thus is clearly informed by #MeToo; the series delves into the lingering trauma of rape, but it also uses Morwenna's story to showcase the patience and compassion of her second husband. This forms an alternative to the kinds of toxic masculinity that often dominate our small screens but also offers the disturbing message that love really does conquer all.

Finally, we return to *Outlander* to discuss a rape survivor who is often absent in popular culture as a whole: the older woman. Most of the rapes we discuss in this book are of young, beautiful women, and as a result, the act of rape, when screened, is often eroticized, the camera lingering on the nubile, desirable body of the victim. However, the rape plots we discuss in this chapter have middle-aged victims, for, just as in real life, the absence of youth does not shield women from sexual violence. This different demographic allows these shows to explore truths about rape that tend to get forgotten on screen: that it is a crime about power and control, not desire. Of course, these shows also tell us a great deal about how aging is viewed in popular culture, much of it problematic. But the rapes of Claire in season 5 of *Outlander*, and of Polly Gray in *Peaky Blinders* (2013–) are focused around the punishment of women who have worked hard to achieve respect and success—and who also are seen to be sexually active even while menopausal. These plotlines show attempts to undermine and punish these subversive middle-aged women, while showing their survival, and also reminding us of the ubiquity of rape; its victims are not protected by their age, any more than they are by their social class and status.

In the last few years, following #MeToo, the extent of the problem of rape has been acknowledged in a way it was not before. The unmasking of high-profile predators has made everyone aware of the problem sexual violence has so long posed in our society, and it is beginning to break the silence and shame that has surrounded this crime for centuries. Sadly, that does not mean that we lose our old assumptions and prejudices, nor that conviction rates improve, overnight. It will be even longer before society's behavior changes in ways that mean rape is no longer tolerated at all. The dramas we explore here were having these conversations long before they became mainstream in other media. Many of these revealed an attempt to show us the brutality of the past and make us thankful for the progress of the present. Unfortunately, that progress is limited at best, for it presupposes a system that polices and punishes rape properly. As the contemporary shows and films we touch on in this book are aware, that is not the system we currently have. Period drama avoids legal responses and offers us instead antiquated or downright inappropriate solutions, usually versions of romance, revenge, or marriage. Many of these are deeply problematic, and all suggest that solutions are in the hands of individuals, when in fact rape should be an issue for society and the state. But by its constant, repeated representation of rape, even in dramas otherwise rose-tinted, this genre does something important. It says: this has always happened to people, throughout history; it happens to all ages, classes, and nationalities, and we have ignored it long enough.

Chapter 1

Rape Fantasy and the "Lawless" Eighteenth Century
Poldark *and* Banished

Period drama's acknowledgment of the historical pervasiveness of rape is itself ideologically significant and, from the point of view of the anti-rape feminist movement, positive, even if the ways in which those rapes are represented are, by turns, gratuitous, problematic, or sensationalized. The rape plotlines in *Poldark* (2015–2019) and *Banished* (2015), which we will examine here, mostly take place prior to #MeToo and offer a pre-watershed insight into a time when rape could still be romanticized and eroticized in a way which might not, or at least should not, be possible after October 2017. At the same time, however, they opened up conversations about consent, rape myths, and rape fantasy and hence form part of the dialogue and increasingly public awareness about sexual violence which made #MeToo possible in the first place. Moreover, they continue to be viewed (via streaming), be discussed online (on fan sites), and have repercussions within the plots of the shows themselves, and thus can be regarded as a reflection of ongoing conversations about and reaction to rape, over this period of dramatic social change.

In narrowing our focus to these two shows that are set in the eighteenth century, we leave behind the confines of the Victorian and Edwardian London town house and country estate that typically have been the settings for most TV period dramas. *Poldark*'s "wild, passionate" (Mosely 2013) Cornish coast and *Banished*'s penal colony of New South Wales instead provide backdrops described by their series' writers as "lawless" and so their acts of sexual violence are presented as an inevitable and endemic part of their environments that supposedly further add to the "authenticity" of the period and help them escape criticisms. The "consensual ravishment" they represent, however, is both typical of eighteenth-century rape culture and still endemic in the twentieth and twenty-first centuries, as we will discuss. Like dramas set in the nineteenth century, those we examine here seek many things from their rape plotlines, which range from the mercenary—ratings and media attention—to the political—commentary on gender, power, and punishment for rape. In both cases, however, narratives of sexual violence, perhaps more than any other plot, allow period dramas to establish a self-aware relationship with the viewer. Part of our discussion, therefore, involves fan responses to the rape narratives in these dramas. While not a scientific analysis, our survey of Facebook and Twitter posts, YouTube tributes, and message boards reveals multiple readings by fans of these rape narratives which do not always align with academic feminist criticisms of these shows. This is most clearly demonstrated by the rape plotline in one of the most-watched period dramas on British television: *Poldark*, in which the titular character enters his former fiancée Elizabeth's home and takes what the latter says "was not rightly his." This scene poses a dilemma for feminist scholars like ourselves; while we read Ross's actions as rape, we find ourselves at odds with what the media and fans in 2016 dubbed more benignly a "bedroom encounter" and even, disturbingly, rewarded it with a top spot on a list of ten "fan favorite TV moments" of that year (*Radio Times* 2016).

THE PROBLEM OF *POLDARK*

Over multiple novels published between 1945 and 2002, *Poldark*'s creator Winston Graham explored the consequences of his hero's invasion of Elizabeth's bedroom, in which he pinned her to the bed and ignored her cries of "Stop, stop I tell you" (Graham 1953: 314). As we have explored elsewhere (Taddeo 2014), the first TV adaptation's fade-out of that moment left enough ambiguity that the act was consensual and viewers returned for the second season, recalling years later on message boards that Elizabeth (Jill Townsend), not Ross (Robin Ellis), was largely in the wrong. But not all fans of the series who read Graham's novels and/or watched that adaptation, either at the time it first aired in 1975 or years later on VHS or DVD, excused Ross's behavior, and concerns were raised on social media prompting the writers of the most recent TV adaptation to reinterpret that scene for twenty-first-century viewers. Having realized after the first season aired in 2015 just how popular the latest BBC adaptation of *Poldark* had become, due in part to lead actor Aidan Turner's sex appeal, head writer Debbie Horsfield needed to tackle what one BBCTV message board post called "the Very Bad Thing that happened in Book 4." Horsfield ultimately reasoned that

> although he is hot-headed and reckless—in the books and as depicted on screen—Ross is fundamentally a man of honor, a rebel who stands up for the

underdog. How likely is it that he would commit a crime against a woman, a woman he has loved for ten years? It would fly in the face of everything we know about him. (quoted in Dickson 2016)

And so, we get a tweaked version of that night that blurred the lines yet again so viewers could choose to believe Ross is not a rapist and that it is Elizabeth who is to blame for all that follows (with some fans calling actress Heida Reed's Elizabeth a "homewrecker" in their Facebook posts).

Indeed, the buildup to the 2016 scene makes Elizabeth appear complicit in what the writers are clearly trying to present as an "affair" (Taddeo 2019): as Ross furiously rides to Trenwith, she is shown at her vanity table, brushing her hair, smiling, likely expecting Ross after sending him news of her engagement to George Warleggan. But when he kicks open the door to her home, she becomes genuinely frightened; he prowls aggressively around her bedroom, tells her she cannot marry George, "my greatest enemy," and grabs her chin and neck to kiss her roughly. She pushes him away and backs toward the bed, cornered, and when she looks behind her at the bed, saying, "You would not dare," he replies, "Oh, I would Elizabeth," and shoving her onto the bed, concludes, "and so would you." After another rough kiss, she kisses back, arching her neck in such a way as to suggest consent, and as his hand reaches under her skirt, she moans as the camera fades out (See figure 1.1). The next morning, she lies naked under the sheets, blissful, as Ross hurriedly dresses, avoiding her question, "What shall we . . . ?"

Fan reaction was divided: on Twitter several posts complained that the BBC was glamorizing rape, while on other sites, fans interpreted the event mainly through its impact on Ross's wife, Demelza, as the one most wronged in this triangle. Others defended Ross by arguing that "love is complicated" and he was a "man driven by his passionate nature" (YouTube). Some state unequivocally, "Ross did not rape Elizabeth, SHE ENJOYED EVERY MOMENT OF IT" (YouTube). And even those who share Demelza's anger seemed to be more disappointed in Ross—"Ross was my Mr. Darcy until that night with Elizabeth"—than sympathetic toward Elizabeth, who was instead condemned as "narcissistic" by many fans (YouTube).

There are clearly problems surrounding the BBC's representation of this plotline, which somehow loses sight of what Graham called "the status of women issue," along the way turning it into something viewers could enjoy as a "complicated" "bedroom encounter" (Taddeo 2014: 209). Fundamentally, as anti-rape campaigners in Britain complained, this new version of the plot perpetuated an outdated rape fantasy. A critic for *The Telegraph* asked, "In whose world was that consensual?" noting that the scene which its writers thought would be more in line with twenty-first-century ideas of "correct behavior" actually opened "the door for the classic rapist's defense: 'she was

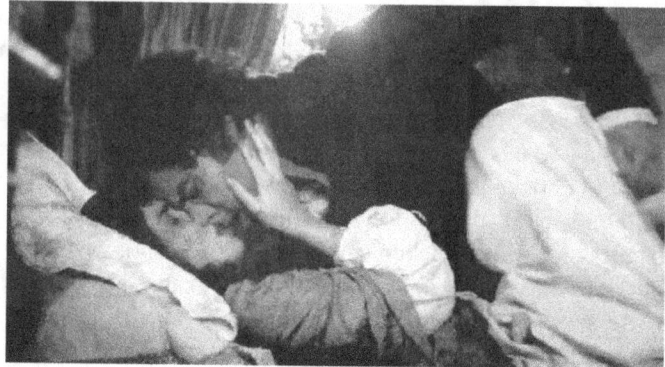

Figure 1.1 The "Bedroom Encounter" in *Poldark*, Episode 2:8 (2016). *Source*: Screen grab by Julie Anne Taddeo.

saying no but she really meant yes, m'lud'" (O'Donovan, 2016). This is, as Sarah Green, codirector at charity End Violence against Women, has pointed out, "a really appalling message. [. . .] They have made the representation of non-consensual sex ambiguous by making her appear to change her mind" (BBC News 2016). Such scenes can be considered ideologically and actually dangerous, given that research into the effects of watching violence on television has indicated that this kind of representation of consensual ambiguity is especially problematic (even more so than more violent rape on screen) given its justification of sexually predatory behavior. As Gunter and Harrison (2001: 122) note, "One particularly important factor [in influencing the viewer] is whether during the course of the rape, the victim becomes sexually aroused." Indeed, one of the most significant problems considered to be caused by the pornography industry is its "portrayals of women expressing pleasure while being aggressed against," which encourages viewers to learn "that aggression during a sexual encounter is pleasure-enhancing for both men and women" (Bridges et al., 2015). *Poldark* is hardly porn, but pleasure and force are bound up here together in problematic ways. And certainly, a viewer would find it difficult to recognize Elizabeth as a victim or to take her "no" seriously given that she appears to have ultimately enjoyed the encounter. Thus, it becomes what Lee Ellis describes as a "positive-outcome rape scene" and therefore more likely to make male viewers "more accepting of rape myths" and more likely to commit rape (1989: 39). In this regard, the show does seem to perpetuate outdated stereotypes about the changeability of female consent, wrapped up in the glossy packaging of highly emotionally charged sex between two attractive people.

That said, however, we cannot entirely dismiss this, *Poldark*'s most controversial plotline, as anti-feminist on these terms. For one thing, the "encounter" itself did create useful and important dialogue in the media and among fans around consent, and we might add that this is especially significant given the kind of sex this is. Nonconsensual intercourse between two people who know and are attracted to each other, and with some lack of clarity around desire and assent, is the kind of sex not often recognized as rape on our screens (usually some variation of "stranger rape"). It is, however, the kind of sex which currently poses the biggest problem under the law and in our courtrooms.[1] Moreover, there are other aspects of the plotline which need to be considered. Susan Berridge has argued that it is not always helpful to talk in terms of a "good or bad" representation of rape on television, and her argument is worth considering in detail here:

> A critical emphasis on whether individual images are positive or negative seriously limits the scope of enquiry. There are a number of inherent problems with measuring how positive individual images are. [. . .] Firstly, this approach displays a patronizing and overly simplistic notion of viewer identification which ignores the possibility of cross-gender identification and polysemic readings and conceives of a direct cause-and-effect relationship between what viewers watch and how they subsequently behave. Secondly, in this criticism, representations are often divorced from their context leading to incomplete analyses. For example, the ambiguities inherent in long-running series become obscured. (Berridge, 2010: 12)

Berridge's first point seems especially pertinent to *Poldark*, a show whose audience is more likely to be made up of women who clearly see "forced seduction" by Ross as a source of fantasy than by the impressionable young male viewers mentioned by Gunter and Harrison earlier. Of course, rape as a subject of female fantasy is a highly contentious argument in feminist studies: some feminist critics might consider the audience who enjoyed the Ross/Elizabeth encounter as examples of women who have internalized their own patriarchal oppression. *Poldark* hence both reflects and epitomizes questions around agency which go to the heart of fourth-wave feminism (we will return to the question of female fantasy later in connection with *Banished*).

However, Berridge's second argument—that sexual violence in all television series needs to be viewed in the long term, not as a specific incident—is also important to consider here. Initial response to the show cannot deny that most audiences did sympathize with Ross (and Demelza, who accuses Elizabeth, not her husband, of "breaking" their marriage) in the immediate aftermath of "that night," but it could be observed that the plotline is presented in a different light by the long-term repercussions of their encounter, and that might shift viewers' perspective. The reason for Elizabeth's resistance (given that she clearly desires Ross) becomes more clear as it emerges she conceives from this intercourse and must live with the long-term repercussions of that illegitimate pregnancy. These include the continuing deception of her new, and increasingly jealous, husband, her attempt to bring about a premature labor with her second child (to convince Warleggan of her natural predisposition to short pregnancies), and the disastrous consequences of this which led to her death. Taken as a long-running story arc, then, the series reminds us that Elizabeth alone bears the burden of their encounter. In another episode in which she witnesses her husband George, acting in his capacity as local magistrate, condemn a servant girl for smearing the "good name" of her employer's son with an accusation of rape, Elizabeth's disgust with the verdict underscores perhaps her own realization that had she ever sought justice for that night with Ross, she would find none. Yet there are eventual hints (perhaps a rethinking of that night by Horsfield herself) that Ross should be viewed—along with the moral codes of the time—as ultimately responsible for Elizabeth's destruction years later. Indeed, Doctor Enys ruefully observes after Elizabeth's death in series 4, "What killed her was seeded long ago." This cannot but create, as Berridge notes, "ambiguities inherent in a long running series" perhaps not thought apparent if we consider only the initial encounter itself. The viewer's judgment and allegiances hence may change over long-term viewing of the show, as the outpouring of fan grief at Elizabeth's death implies.[2] Indeed, we might add that this gives any televisual representation of rape an added dimension which is lacking in other media: the serial nature of most small screen period dramas (many of which run for three or more TV seasons) afford writers and actors the possibility to investigate the long-term effects of rape, such as victim trauma and recovery, and in *Poldark*'s case a critical reappraisal of the act and perpetrator. Not all shows, however, do share this view of rape as a crime with severe long-term consequences for the victim, as we will see with *Banished*.

"PLEASE MAKE LOVE TO ME": WHEN RAPE BECOMES CONSENT IN *BANISHED*

At first glance no two period dramas could be further apart than *Poldark* and the gritty and grimy *Banished*, BBC2's series about the early days of the British penal colony of New South Wales. These shows have, however, been compared to one another in the press: both were launched the same week and featured a military hero called Ross, and indeed the success of the former show has been held responsible for the failure of the latter to return for a second series (Taylor 2017). The most fundamental similarity between them, however, is in fact a shared representation of sexual violence: as James Ward notes, both shows "are part of a renewed testing of boundaries around consent not just in period drama but more generally in popular culture" (Ward 2018: 31). The "romance" between convict Katherine "Kitty" McVitie (Joanna Vanderham) and Major Robert Ross (Joseph Millson) yet again illustrates "how 'No' is still portrayed to mean 'Yes' in contemporary fiction" (Linton 2015).

In *Banished*, there is a shortage of women in the penal colony, and since the British officers have first "dibs" on the prettiest convicts, Major Ross forces Private MacDonald (Ryan Corr), whom he accuses of having hidden away "Kitty" for his own use, to "loan" her out two nights a week in exchange for a career promotion for MacDonald and a bag of dried peas for Kitty (the convicts are starving). Kitty, sensing that MacDonald is too fearful to say no to his superior (an interesting twist on consent), convinces him that she is willing to do this to ensure their survival in the colony. In her first sexual encounter with Ross (See figure 1.2), Kitty is shown unlacing her dress as he places her arms around his body and kisses her before the fade-out, so that the viewer is left with just enough doubt, since she did not pull away or say "no," that consent was at last achieved. But such doubt should disappear when we see Kitty, visibly upset, later run to the beach to cleanse herself. After several such nights she attempts to drown herself—an act which enrages Ross who asks her (to elicit her and the viewer's sympathy, perhaps) if he is so loathsome that she'd prefer death. Any exploration of the effects of sexual slavery upon the victim is soon left behind, however. Gradually, as she spends more time with Ross, and they exchange stories about their pasts, Kitty begins to soften so that their later encounters are not only consensual (a consent engineered, as Ward notes, by coercion [31]) but more significantly sought after by her; it becomes too easy for the viewer to forget that Kitty, pampered and listened to by Ross in his elegantly decorated tent, is a prisoner, of the British colony and of Ross's manipulation. Finally, Ross no longer wants to give her food for their encounters—"for that would treat you as a whore"—and Kitty assumes these words imply he loves her. In the final episode, she spurns MacDonald and runs to Ross's tent, exclaiming breathlessly, "Please make love to me." The scene that follows, of the two disrobing and her moans of pleasure overheard by MacDonald as he stands outside the tent, seems intended to erase the problematic origins of this "relationship" and reaffirm Kitty's "choice."

The evolution of Kitty's story line, from rape victim to willing lover, differs from that of the other convict, Elizabeth Quinn (MyAnna Buring), who is not allowed to marry fellow prisoner, Thomas Barrett (Julian Rhind-Tutt), because as Major Ross declares, "Convict women belong to my soldiers." Such sexual servitude is illustrated when she is jailed for a minor offense and forced to have sex with Private Buckley in exchange for getting a message to her lover, Tommy. Earlier in another episode, she had fought off Private Buckley who shouted at her, "Just let me do this!"—and eventually she

Figure 1.2 Coerced Consent in *Banished*, Episode 3 (2015). *Source*: Screen grab by Julie Anne Taddeo.

does "let" him—but this too—consent by coercion—is rape. As *Banished*'s creator, Jimmy McGovern, asks of her situation, "If you're a woman and you have nothing except your body, how far do you go to survive?" (quoted in Wilson, 2015). When Buckley loses a card game to Tommy in another episode (in which the stakes are Elizabeth), the former retaliates by bragging about having "had" Elizabeth, prompting Tommy to beat him savagely, eventually leading to Tommy's death at the gallows. Likewise, Private MacDonald, upon hearing his former lover, Kitty, enjoying herself in Major Ross's bed, kills himself on the very beach where Kitty previously tried to drown herself. The fight between men to assert dominance over women's bodies ultimately makes these women complicit in their deaths.

FROM THE EIGHTEENTH CENTURY TO THE TWENTIETH: RAPE FANTASY

What both *Poldark* and *Banished* have in common, then, is they both suggest that women initially resistant to sex can soon be persuaded into pleasure by an attractive man, or, even more disturbing, that control and coercion are ultimately aphrodisiacs (a famous marital rape plot in series 1 of *Game of Thrones* perpetuates the same idea). In this regard they reflect one of the oldest sexual myths, one that has been used through the centuries, to justify rape. Historical fidelity is not necessarily an excuse for perpetuating such messages (as we will discuss further when we examine the many rape plots in *Outlander*), but it is true that these eighteenth-century set shows can be considered an accurate reflection of their contexts. As a number of critics have pointed out, the eighteenth century was a period preoccupied by rape, in which the most popular fiction was filled with tales of women fighting with both male attention and their own desires:

> Rape was everywhere. . . . Eighteenth-century sexual discourse on both perceived normative sexual behaviour and rape circulated in the public domain in mainstream literature, medical and pseudo-medical manuals, and erotic fiction; all buttressed the public view on rape and fed into perceptions of the raped and the rapists. (Mills, 2009: 146)

As Margaret Doody has explored, best-selling novels like Samuel Richardson's *Pamela* (1740) and *Clarissa* (1748), which draw heavily on earlier stories of "love and seduction," display the crossover between rape narratives and erotica at this period (Doody 1974: 128). Nothing was more desirable, for an eighteenth-century readership, than a virtuous woman whose resistance is eventually overcome (even if only, as in Pamela's case, through marriage). By being "ravished" by Ross Poldark, Elizabeth joins a long line of famous literary victims offered up for audience titillation in "cult of seduction" narratives (Hitchcock 1997: 99–100). *Clarissa* is perhaps the most famous example of this: even Ian Watt's influential reading of the novel reads like a justification of the "she wanted it really" defense. Speaking of her ambiguity toward Lovelace, he argues that "we are fully entitled to suspect Clarissa herself of not knowing her own feelings," a shocking negation of woman's ability to know her own mind (Watt 1971: 228–229).

The BBC's *Poldark* is not just a product of its eighteenth-century setting, though, of course. It is also in dialogue with its own, earlier adaptation from the 1970s, a decade when, post-sexual revolution, it became commonplace to talk of women "wanting to be raped." Rape fantasy on screen had already become commonplace by the 1970s but was more usually found in Gothic fiction, where the Hammer horror films of the 1950s and 1960s were filled with images of women fatally seduced by Count Dracula and when the titular heroine of *Rosemary's Baby* appears to enjoy her halogenic impregnation by the devil possessing her husband. From the 1970s on, however, rape fantasy entered the mainstream. This was after all a decade where major Hollywood star Frank Langella, who starred as *Dracula* in the 1979 TV adaptation, could tell *US* magazine that

> Dracula as a character is very erotic. . . . A woman can be totally passive with Dracula: "he made me drink, I couldn't help it." Actually, I can't think of a woman who wouldn't like to be taken if it's with love. If you take a woman by force and at the same time gently, you can't fail. (Sokol, 2019)

We might expect such beliefs to be expressed by men in the 1970s, a decade in which many of the most high-profile stars have since been disgraced for sexual harassment or worse. The idea that women want to be "taken" by force was not only confined to men's problematic imaginations, however. Nancy Friday's seminal *My Secret Garden* famously acknowledged back in 1973 that rape was a commonplace fantasy probably due to its ability to "relieve [women] of responsibility and guilt" (Friday 1996: 108). Hence the coercing or "ravishing" of the heroine has long been "a prevalent subject in popular romance" (Horeck 4). As Karen Chow, writing about female desire in *The Sheik*, notes,

> The initial "rape" scenes participate in a rape fantasy that is a common trope in romance novels—the typically stunning, always desirable hero forces the heroine into sex, an event that, while hardly empowering, allows her to lose her inhibitions without taking moral responsibility for doing so; consequently, the heroine is able to express herself sexually. (1999: 72)

Chow's argument, which could equally be applied to the plots of most Mills and Boon novels of the mid-twentieth century, seems a convincing one. We might expect the need to experience pleasure while being absolved from blame to dominate over all other female concerns through much of the twentieth century, given the difficulties of sex without judgment for women in this period. Even when Wendy Craig infamously declared that she "wanted to be raped" in Carla Lane's sitcom *Butterflies* as late as 1978, she was speaking for a generation of women who wanted to enjoy the fruits of the sexual revolution but still found it impossible to do so guilt-free.

What is more surprising, however, is that the desire for what Leon F. Seltzer thinks should be re-termed "consensual ravishment," or "agreed-to aggression" (to acknowledge that some level of consent is in fact present), seems to have endured even into the more liberated twenty-first century (Seltzer 2014) and even in the #MeToo era. On Twitter, *Banished* fans and "Ross Kittens" long for the return of Major Ross, several years after the show's cancellation, and fans still post memes about offering him sex in exchange for a bag of peas, suggesting they envy Kitty for her situation rather than seeing it as rape. The Ross-Kitty story line is very much presented and consumed as a "love story" rather than an interrogation of British colonialism and sexual slavery. The BBC's accompanying website describes Major Ross's actions in terms of his, not Kitty's, personal development: "He starts a relationship with Kitty initially for sex but he gradually falls in love with her, counter to everything he believes about convicts." As James Ward observes, Major Ross "came to be viewed as an object of straight female desire comparable to Ross Poldark," and on social media, fans reconciled the "loathsome" actions of the character with their attraction to the handsome actor, Joseph Millson, who played him (Ward 29). There were similar viewer responses to the characterization of Jaime Lannister in *Game of Thrones* whose rape of his sister (following a long redemption arc) proved difficult for many fans (Quora, 2016).

These stories epitomize ideas that are foundational to the modern rape culture we unconsciously imbibe and many condone, and these ideas bleed into real-life and legal attitudes to sexual violence. These shows can thus be considered recent examples of the rape fantasy. Indeed, the huge success of E. L. James's *Fifty Shades of Grey* (2015) novels and their film adaptations suggests that fantasies of domination and relinquished control remain bankable "as a way of understanding and navigating post-feminist sexualized culture" while "providing a conduit for readers to explore their own sexual agency" (Tripodi 2017: 94). As Sarah Stevens has explored, these texts, despite their flaws, are important because they have encouraged discourse around kink and the nature of female desire:

> Many voices are now emerging that engage feminist discourse on BDSM and kink from both scholarly and practical perspectives. The traditional feminist narratives of BDSM "matching" patriarchal ideals are undone by a rise in submissive practitioners who additionally identify as feminists and consider feminism to motivate the ethics used in their BDSM practice and in the representations they create. *50 Shades of Grey* has been a catalyst in the proliferation of such voices in the debate. (2014)

In this regard, it is reductive to sit in feminist judgment over texts which explore female pleasure, but, then, as Stevens points out, "the concept of pleasure, and its ability to evade politics, has long been a fraught feminist issue" (2014). The debates that have surrounded *Fifty Shades* reveal the extent to which these issues remain deeply problematic to some feminists. Many of them simply regard the novels as misleading appropriations of BDSM culture, but for others, "pleasure in (female) masochism has, for obvious reasons, been questioned as to whether it is pleasure at all" (Williams, 1989: 210). We have discussed *Fifty Shades* here as one of the most talked-about recent examples of these issues, but in fact even James's controversial novels do not take their consent-related plotlines as far as *Banished* or *Poldark*. James's protagonist may be manipulated and controlled in her pursuit of pleasure but is truly a neoliberal heroine: her enslavement is her own choice, and her lover is so preoccupied with her consent that he famously obtains it in writing.

The period dramas discussed here go one step further, perhaps using their textual distance from the more politically correct present, in order to more fully uncover or exploit the viewer's fascination with, or desire for, what we may politely term "ravishment." Of course, it is unsurprising that the whole notion of rape fantasy has long been "a thorn in [second-wave] feminism's side" because "the idea that women secretly fantasize about sexual violation has been grounds for dismissing women's charges of rape in the legal arena" (Horeck 4). Yet for many sex-positive feminists rape fantasy is just that: fantasy, not reality. For them, women's interests in these nonconsensual scenes are part of the exploration of their erotic imagination. Susie Bright, for example, has written about reclaiming her own sexuality through rape fantasy in her book *Sexual Reality* (1992). Noah Berlatsky, in her essay about Nancy Friday in *The Atlantic*, however, complicates this. She points out that, as many women have rape fantasies and many women have experienced sexual violence, the two will necessarily overlap, with perhaps deeply problematic consequences for the survivor's mental health and the shame and guilt she experiences: "If in some sense her fantasy helps her deal with her assault ... it's also the case that in some sense her fantasy *is* the assault" (2013).

There is no easy answer to such debates, but irrespective of the stance we choose to take on them, the existence of the fan base for *Poldark*'s and *Banished*'s male leads—and the highly romantic and often pornographic fan fiction writing they have inspired—suggests that rape fantasy is enduring and powerful. Moreover, it seems to be in period drama that it finds its most mainstream expression.[3] As Claire Monk has acknowledged, after all, "The potential erotic attractions of some heritage films are very evident": she cites "online fan/audience discussions" as evidence and quotes from viewers who enjoy period drama because it constructs "desire as something transgressive and dangerous" (Monk 2011: 153). Historical fictions clearly allow audiences to explore their desire for all that is illicit and taboo. For some, that is merely sex which would be commonplace today in our "hookup" culture, made enjoyably "transgressive" by the expectations and repressions of an earlier time. For others, however, that is the pleasures offered by witnessing something rather darker: "consensual ravishment," as we might term it, on screen. Perhaps under the cover of the distance provided by the costume, manners, and mores of very different eras, women can acknowledge desire in much more controversial ways.

It is important to recognize, however, that these types of plotlines in period dramas may have more adverse effects on some viewers. Phoebe Linton (2015), in a review of *Banished*, warned that "generations of young or adolescent girls—and boys—are having their formative ideas and experiences of romance molded by these images of sex and violence we leave dangerously unquestioned." Indeed, five years after Linton's review, the Essential Research study in 2020 surveyed more than 1,000 adults in Australia and found that 42 percent of men aged between eighteen and thirty-four do not regard physical violence such as punching or hitting to be "domestic violence" and 44 percent of them believed nonconsensual sexual activity as also beyond the confines of what constitutes "domestic violence" (Tu 2020). In 2019, the British government addressed demands that children younger than fifteen should not be exposed to rape scenes on film or TV—curiously, one of the films that prompted an outcry from parents was the 2008 eighteenth-century set film, *The Duchess* (whose brutal marital rape scene is discussed in chapter 6). But placing a "fifteen" rather than a "twelve" rating on films to restrict viewing by age does little to alter the way the rape is presented on our screens in the first place, and when surveyed, the majority of the 10,000 parents replied that they were worried about "the sexualization of society and what they called the pornification of society" rather than how these films were impacting younger viewers' understanding of rape or consent (BBC News 2019).

We have concentrated on eighteenth-century period drama in this chapter, but other recent shows are also implicated in perpetuating this idea that women want to be ravished and that "no" really means "yes." Lady Mary's (Michelle Dockery) infamous encounter with visiting Turkish diplomat Kemal Pamuk (Theo James) in series 1 of *Downton Abbey* is another example of the continuing social acceptability of "agreed-to-aggression." This plotline has Pamuk enter her bedroom unexpectedly late at night, and then half-persuade, half-blackmail Mary to have sex with him:

Mary: "You must be mad . . . please leave! I'll scream!"
Pamuk: "No you won't."
Mary: "I'll ring the bell . . ."
Pamuk: "And will you really let [the hallboy] find a man in your room?"
Mary: "I'd be ruined if they even knew we'd had this conversation. . . . I'm not what you think I am. If I've led you on, I'm sorry but I'm not . . . no, I've never done anything like this." (*Downton*, series 1 episode 3)

Lady Mary clearly feels guilty for flirting with Pamuk at dinner, as though doing so committed her to something more. She is attracted to him, but he is not offering marriage, and like *Poldark*'s Elizabeth she is all too aware of the implications this could have for her future if she is caught. Such risks, she implies, are hardly worth a few minutes of pleasure. And, like Elizabeth, she is correct to be worried, for the consequences of this "encounter" will dog her and her family for years to come. It is notable, however, that audience and critical response to this plotline focused not on the coercion of Mary but the death of Pamuk in her bed, and the half-Gothic, half-comic removal of his body. Even *The Guardian* joked about this incident (Groskop 2015) which the *Daily Mail* described as a "racy exploit" rather than rape, and fan websites which respond to it are more preoccupied about whether it leaves Mary a virgin for future husband Matthew than whether or not she was assaulted

(DowntonAbbeyFandom.com 2013). Clearly, the idea that women are ultimately happy to be bullied into sex has not been left in the 1790s, nor the 1970s, but continues on our screens today.

CONCLUSION

This chapter focuses on two shows set in the "lawless" eighteenth century, but the themes it describes are far from confined to this period. In *Poldark* and *Banished*, rape is as much about the male actor's desirability, male identity, and rivalry for ownership of women's bodies, as about the actual, female victims of the crime. In *Poldark*, Elizabeth becomes collateral damage in the ongoing war between Ross and his nemesis Warleggan who are continually clashing over politics, law, and land, as well as women. Warleggan even boasts to his uncle upon marriage to Elizabeth that he is now "in possession of the field [. . .] of the woman he [Ross] loved." In *Banished*, the Kitty/Ross/MacDonald triangle is presented as a power struggle between soldiers which eventually ends when the loser, Kitty's former lover MacDonald, shoots himself. This use of rape as a way of articulating male anxiety and rivalries is far from unique to period drama and is of course not the only use to which a rape plotline can be put. As Sarah Projansky notes, rape has been utilized as a narrative device in many ways. Writing of television and film generally, she observes that it can be the "precipitation and sometimes justification of a more violent, more social, more narratively significant conflict" or, as here, used "to focus on relationships between men" (Projansky 2001: 63). What all these conventions of the plot share, of course, is that in some way, the plight of the victim takes a back seat to, or is forced to make room for, the agenda of patriarchy. We could argue here, then, that the real issue we should have with rape plotlines is not how sensational or unnecessary they are but that actually they all too often are more interested in a male body politic than the traumatized female body—a subject we will explore in a later chapter.

We have also discussed in this chapter the way scenes like Ross Poldark's "ravishment" of Elizabeth have been represented, and understood by fans, as romantic or erotic. For sex-positive feminists, such fan responses could be interpreted as the playful exploration of submission and domination within the "safe space" of television period drama. The problem is, however, that such erotic possibilities are overshadowed by the many real-life crimes which took place then and now, and society's continuing condoning and overlooking of them. After this scene, Ross asks his wife Demelza (and notably not Elizabeth, the true victim of his actions) "for some understanding, knowing you as I do." Indeed, knowing his wife (and Turner knowing his adoring and desiring fans), Ross expects and receives, if not forgiveness, at least an acceptance, explaining away his actions as a moment of "madness." Perhaps this makes sense for the series' eighteenth-century context (when "temporary madness" and "lust" were actual legal defenses)—and even for its pre-#MeToo screen date. Hopefully, though, in future such "understanding" will be directed not to the perpetrators of sexual violence but to their victims and to the wider structures which have made rape commonplace and unpunished for so long.

NOTES

1. See, for example, the debates around, and the extensive media coverage of, the recent Ulster rugby rape trial, https://www.independent.co.uk/voices/northern-ireland-ulster-rugby-rape-trial-not-guilty-im-with-her-a8280066.html (accessed October 4, 2018).

2. See sampling of fan reactions to Elizabeth's death in season 4 at https://www.whatsontv.co.uk/news/poldark-star-reaction-fans-response-characters-death-548037 (accessed 4 October 2018).

3. See *Banished* Fan Fiction samples at https://www.fanfiction.net/tv/Banished/ (accessed October 10, 2018).

Chapter 2

Rape Responses, Romance, and Rape-Revenge

Before period drama began to put a huge range of rapes on our televisions, the main way sexual violence was viewed on screen was via that long-popular genre, the rape-revenge film. From the earliest days of talking cinema (Hitchcock's *Blackmail*, 1929) to the genre's heyday in 1970s horror (*I Spit on Your Grave* in 1978, and many others since) these films shared a similar plot: a young woman is raped, but survives and then tracks down, often tortures, and finally kills her attacker or attackers in revenge for what they have done to her. Many of these films have been criticized for displaying graphic sexual violence and being primarily interested in rape only as a catalyst which sets more gratuitous violence in motion for the viewer's pleasure (Ebert, 1980). That said, as critics like Jacinda Read have observed, "The rape-revenge cycle can be seen as one of the privileged sites through and against which meanings of feminism are played out" (2000: 72). Earlier examples (like *The Birth of a Nation* and the aforementioned *Blackmail*) may have often used these plots to reassert and police traditional feminine values and female behavior, but post-1970s rape-revenge, in particular, interacted with second-wave feminism in important ways. These films displayed both the trauma and horror of the crime and made apparent the need for personal, vigilante justice, given that legal recompense was, and indeed still is, failing rape survivors.

Rape-revenge has endured, in various forms, to the present day: satirical psychological thriller *Promising Young Woman* (directed by Emerald Fennell, 2020) is just the most recent example of this successful genre: "It's another entry in a growing trend of rape-revenge films that venture outside of horror to deliver a provocative critique of modern rape culture" (Navarro, 2021). Winner of Best Screenplay at the 2021 Oscars, this film reworks old tropes by following the revenge exacted by Cassie, a young woman (Carey Mulligan) whose best friend has killed herself after being publicly raped—and filmed—by popular students at a college party years before. Cassie has given her life over to vengeance, pretending to be drunk and vulnerable at bars and then threatening and intimidating the predatory men who try to have sex with her. Later she targets for revenge those involved in, or complicit in, her friend's rape, which it turns out is most of the people they knew at college. As we will discuss later, one of the most common themes in post-#MeToo rape on screen is an acknowledgment that rape is not an individual's problem but is facilitated by a whole society. In this film, women—from the dean of the university downward—as well as men have contributed to this rape culture by supporting the perpetrators, judging the victim, or simply remaining silent about what they know. Through the threat of violence, Cassie is able to "educate" many of them about their complicity, and finally to exact revenge on the rapist himself, but she pays for this with her death. The film reminds us that proper justice for rape is still elusive, for the perpetrators are finally arrested for the murder of Cassie not for the rape itself: she has sacrificed herself, and the film's happy ending, to ensure they end up in jail. In this society, Fennell implies, murder is the only crime against women which the law takes at all seriously.

If the highly educated, middle-class heroines in *Promising Young Woman* cannot achieve legal justice for rape, violent revenge is certainly the only option for nineteenth-century Irish servant Claire, the rape survivor in recent period thriller *The Nightingale* (Jennifer Kent 2019) set in Tasmania in 1825. Unlike Fennell's film, however, the rape, perpetuated by a number of British soldiers, is screened, in a brutal five-minute-long scene which proved grueling for many viewers, some of who left the cinema unable to continue watching (Harmon 2019). Kent defended the violent scenes in the film as the "honest and necessary" representation of real life atrocity; however, she added, "If we showed what really happened in Tasmania in 1825, no audience could bear it" (Kent quoted in Harmon, 2019). This film shows how this genre can be put to new use from an intersectional perspective as a condemnation of the colonialism and white privilege that goes hand in hand with sexual violence. It also, of course, shows how rape-revenge film can be reworked as historical fiction, too: Kent's film has been lauded as a reminder of the horrors of the past and the continuing suffering and injustices of the present.

RAPE, REVENGE, AND MALE IDENTITY ON TELEVISION

Given the continuing popularity of rape-revenge as a genre on the big screen, then, we might expect many of the rapes in televisual period drama to follow this formula. Rather disturbingly, however, those rapes we explore here do not feature angry women seeking justice: in those small screen rapes that *are* avenged, it is the husband or lover who exacts revenge on the rapist. As Sarah Projansky notes in *Watching Rape*, the crime often serves as the excuse to indulge in "a particularly violent version of masculinity" in which the victimized women become mere "props" in the narrative (2001: 60). This kind of narrative pattern has also been present in many historical films: for example, in that most masculine of genres, the traditional Western, "the outraged who seek vengeance for rape are typically the husbands or fiancés of the victim rather than the victim herself" (Read: 125). However, as Read goes on to note, post-1970 Westerns often move "women from the margins of the western's symbolic world to its frontier," and thus more recent examples of the genre like *The Quick and the Dead* (1995) explore women exacting revenge on their attackers (125). In this regard, then, the contemporary period television we explore here is rather more conservative, and even anti-feminist, than the big screen, for it cannot imagine a female rape survivor seeking her own justice. And this is only the tip of the iceberg when we consider how period dramas, in focusing on male revenge, often become much more about the journey, development, and gender identity of the male lead than they are about the victim, and it is really this problem that we explore in this chapter.

Back in the 1990s, Lisa M. Cuklanz criticized prime-time television for using the rape of women primarily as a means of expressing concerns about masculinity and exploring plotlines around men:

> Programs . . . treat the subject of rape in ways that highlight masculine attitudes, postures, behaviors, values and feelings. Women's reactions, though not entirely eliminated, are peripheral in such episodes. . . . Rather than pushing these male characters to the sidelines, the subject of rape seems to be used to throw them into high relief, often contrasting a protagonist's enlightened and sensitive approach to rape with the confused and outmoded attempts of others, including rapists . . . marginalizing rape victims and other women in the process. (Cuklanz, 1999, 63)

The period dramas we have been examining in this book, all produced more than two decades since Cuklanz's assessment, reflect how this rape trope has persisted even into the twenty-first century. This is all the more surprising given this is a genre that has always had a largely female fan base and women-driven narratives and from which we could expect better. This chapter will put several such rapes in conversation with each other: *Downton Abbey*'s rape of Anna Bates, Carolyn Bligh's in *A Place to Call Home*, Monika's rape in *Ku'damm 56* (2016–), and Brianna's rape in *Outlander*. The first three rapes aired on the eve of #MeToo but continue to reach large audiences via streaming sites such as Amazon and Netflix; as such, reactions to the rapes may vary over time, but the focus of this chapter will be how the rapes were presented and received by critics and fans in their particular moment. Yet, as we will see in the case of *Outlander*'s rape, even though it was filmed with #MeToo in mind, the impact of the rape on the victim continues to take a back seat to a male revenge scenario.

"THE POOR MAN'S HEART IS BREAKING FOR NOT KNOWING": RAPE IN *DOWNTON ABBEY*

Season 4's beating and rape of Anna Bates (Joanne Froggatt) by visiting valet, Mr. Green (Nigel Harman), was a seminal moment in *Downton Abbey*, garnering intense criticism from TV critics and fans alike. We have discussed this plotline elsewhere (Byrne, 2015) but so significant was this rape in cultural consciousness that we must revisit it here in some detail. In Britain, the scene prompted over 200 complaints to ITV and media regulator Ofcom (Halliday 2013), and the day after the episode aired on American PBS stations across the country, *The Washington Post* declared it was out of sync with the overall tone of a series that "at its core is about fluff, frivolity and fabulous fashion" (Heim 2014). Another critic for *The Guardian* noted, "Raped women are not objects to be used to shake up a dull plot or add juice to a sanguine character" (Cosslett and Bidisha 2013). In fact, as we have noted elsewhere, a TV series about servants would be remiss to omit a rape plotline (Byrne, 2015: 182), but like Brianna's rape by the pirate Bonnet in season 5 of *Outlander*, Anna's promoted the myth of stranger rape when in real life the greatest threat to a servant would be within the domestic setting by someone known to her. Of course, in *Downton*, the rapist would have to be an outsider because after three seasons, the public had grown to love the Abbey's men, both upstairs and down, none of whom—rather unrealistically—had ever subjected the female staff to sexual harassment or violence.

The series was careful to warn viewers of upcoming violence in the episode before it aired at 9:00 p.m. Occurring mostly off-screen as the family and servants watch the performance of opera singer Dame Kiri Te Kanawa, the viewer is shown enough violence to dispel any notion of consent. Mr. Green strikes Anna and drags her to the back room as her screams are muffled by the opera singer above stairs, and in the aftermath we see Anna in a state of shock, her face bruised and lip cut, her hair and dress disheveled. What some critics saw as a "cheap ratings stunt" or even Fellowes's attempt to be a bit "anti-Downton" himself prompted a defense by the series' creator and lead writer:

Rape Responses, Romance, and Rape-Revenge

Figure 2.1 Mrs. Hughes Comforts Anna After Her Rape by Mr. Green in *Downton Abbey*, Episode 4:3 (2014). *Source*: Screen grab by Julie Anne Taddeo.

> If we'd wanted a sensational rape we could have stayed down in the kitchen with the camera during the whole thing and wrung it out. The point of our handling is not that we're interested in sensationalizing but we're interested in exploring the mental damage and the emotional damage. (Fellowes, quoted in Wyatt 2013)

Also proud of the series' handling of the story line, Joanne Froggatt, in the role of Anna, "felt a big responsibility to get it right" but added that it was important to see the scene in its historical context:

> It was set 100 years ago when women felt unable to tell the police about sexual assaults. There was still such a stigma attached to any kind of attack like this that you were very much in danger of losing all of that.... If a woman lost her reputation that would bring shame upon the house, she could lose her job, she could lose her husband. And society still saw it as no smoke without fire, "well he's only a man—he couldn't help himself." (quoted in Halliday 2013)

Indeed, Anna's ensuing self-blame (was she too friendly? she wonders) as well as her confiding in housekeeper Mrs. Hughes (See figure 2.1) after the rape, who reassures Anna of her blamelessness, resonated with many female viewers, suggesting that perhaps not much had changed (in terms of attitudes) in the 100 years since *Downton*'s setting. Froggatt heard from victims who told her they no longer felt alone—some even said they were able to share their experience of sexual violence for the very first time. Writing the next day for Bustle.com (which bills itself as "the premier digital destination for young women"), Rachel Semigran (2013) echoed such a reaction:

> I could go on for ages about the overarching metaphor of a woman not being heard despite her screaming—that Anna was literally in the basement of the lower class, representing just how low women are regarded. I could go on and on about how Anna's shame is representative of how rape victims are made to feel about themselves. About how Green so succinctly expelled the forceful entitlement rapists feel over their victims. But then I think about the way Anna clutched to her stomach, knowing what was there, and my heart ached.

As Nickie D. Phillips points out, and as we will see elsewhere in this book, when rape occurs in popular TV programs, phone calls to rape crisis hotlines spike (2017: 95). In this regard, even a series like *Downton*, often faulted for being conservative in its sexual politics, can be empowering for its viewers. To be clear, there was/is no single reaction to scenes such as Mr. Green's rape of Anna Bates. Some fans said they would not tune in again, but future ratings for the series remained healthily in the millions. One such fan, a rape survivor, tweeted that she had hoped *Downton* would be for her a "safe fluffy space" and felt betrayed by this episode. But period drama has never been a "safe space" when it comes to sexual violence, as this book shows: in six decades and counting, rape has been a constant theme in period TV adaptations, and when presented in a genre that is women-focused in its narrative and viewership, rape, while not the only story told about women's lives, cannot and should not be absent. American viewer and feminist blogger Linda Lowen adds that Anna's rape was crucial not just to bringing light to the real histories of domestic servants who were routinely subjected to rape and harassment but to ending the stigma of sexual violence in contemporary Western culture:

> RAINN (Rape, Abuse & Incest National Network) reminds us that every two minutes, another American is being sexually assaulted. The next time you watch *Downton Abbey*, 30 individuals will be victimized as Anna was victimized. We'll never see their agony or know their faces. Is it too much to ask of any of us to bear witness to just one survivor's pain and efforts to return to a life of wholeness? (2013)

And so, as Lowen concludes, whatever Fellowes's motivation in including the rape of Anna Bates, whom many fans regarded as a member of their Sunday night family, it succeeded in stimulating awareness and debate, in online forums like Twitter, at dinner parties, and at work.

There were many positive outcomes, then, associated with the screening of Anna's rape and the discourse it produced. As with most of the rape plotlines in this book, however, there are still problematic implications for real-life survivors who, after telling their stories, do not get the same response Anna does. That her rape *is* unquestioningly believed by the other characters in the show, for example, is of course sadly far from the experience of most real-life victims. In Anna's case, however, her story is readily believable because it fits the criteria for "real rape": as we mention earlier, Anna is beaten before the attack and bears the visible marks of violence afterward. Of course, physical violence and sexual violence do frequently go together, but just as often do not, and one of our society's most damaging assumptions is that a crime without evidence of resistance is not a true rape. (This perpetuation of the myth of rape as a violent crime, committed by an evil outsider, may make the sexual violence in other shows where there are no bloodied lips or bruised backs more difficult for fans to accept as true "rape": we examined two such plotlines, in *Poldark* and *Banished*, in chapter 1.)

Furthermore, just as her rape is the "right" kind of rape, Anna is the right "type" of victim to be believed and to provoke sympathy and outrage on her behalf. She is after all (in contrast to many other victims who are greeted with a less sympathetic response) modestly dressed, devoted to her husband, and sober (the fact she leaves the performance because of a headache, an age-old excuse for women avoiding sex, may have been used to further reinforce her chastity and lack of sexual interest on this occasion). This all constructs her as a reliable witness and blameless victim, and she is rewarded by being believed by her colleagues and (later on) her employers, even if they do not consider actually calling the police. It may be a positive thing to show survivors like Anna being believed, but that she is can be regarded as yet another example of *Downton*'s determination to "rose-tint" the past. Just as the show glosses over the historical reality that it would be more likely for a servant to be raped by an upper-class member of her own household, it also avoids acknowledging that, as that servant, Anna would be unlikely to have her story heard in any way. The unquestioning support she receives conceals the real-life reality that, in the 1920s and today, rape survivors from certain backgrounds are much less likely to be taken seriously when they report their attack:

> As Kimberlé Crenshaw (1991) famously argued, only an intersectional analysis that considers gender alongside other vectors of power such as race and class is capable of analysing the ways in which public credibility and sympathy is denied to women of colour, working class and other marginalised women. Sweeping claims of a new era of belief for women's testimony are only tenable . . . in the absence of an intersectional lens. (Andersson et al., 2019)

By suggesting that "genuine" rapes—and the viewer knows that Anna was beaten and did not consent, as they have themselves witnessed it—will be unquestioningly believed, *Downton* is ignoring the disturbing fact that this has not been, and is not still, the reality for many women, especially working-class women like Anna and women of color.

This is not the only issue with Anna's rape plot, of course. As we mention earlier, Fellowes may have suggested that what the show was really interested in was "exploring the mental . . . and emotional damage" rape can cause, but in fact what he really means is the emotional damage inflicted on *the victim's husband*. The episodes that followed Anna's rape, unfortunately but not surprisingly, shifted narrative focus away from her and toward Mr. Bates (Brendan Coyle). Even in the immediate aftermath of the rape, Anna's first thought is not about herself but about her husband, as she tells Mrs. Hughes (Phyllis Logan) that if he learns the truth, he will want revenge and thus endanger himself (Mr. Bates already had one arrest in his past). Urging Anna to let her husband know why she is acting withdrawn and avoiding his touch, Mrs. Hughes pleads, "The poor man's heart is breaking for not knowing," to which Anna replies, "Better a broken heart than a broken neck." Not only does Anna wish to protect Bates from the gallows, however, she is also worried that the rape of his wife would further the feelings of emasculation which have already resulted from his physical disability and a career in service to others. Bates's jealousy had already been provoked, as Green intended, when he saw the latter chatting with his wife and later, just before he rapes her, Green cruelly draws attention to her husband's "deficiencies," insinuating "it was time she had a real man who could make her happy." When she at last tells her husband of the rape, without revealing the assailant's identity, Mr. Bates immediately turns the attention away from his wife to himself, blaming himself for not being there to protect her, and then, as predicted and feared by his wife, expressing his desire for revenge. The story line then becomes a rape-revenge plot, as Mr. Green is murdered off-screen (he is pushed into oncoming traffic, presumably, we learn in another episode, by one of his other victims). And, as with earlier examples of rape-revenge film, the rape in this show is then thrust aside, becoming merely a catalyst for another plot entirely: a murder mystery. Amid the police investigation of Anna and Bates, and their struggles to prove themselves innocent, the focus on the rape itself is entirely lost.

This treatment of a rape plot is far from unique to *Downton*. *Time* magazine writer Graeme Macmillan (2014), for example, described the aftermath of Anna's ordeal as "fridging"—"the practice of doing something horrific or tragic to a female character with the sole objective of causing an emotional reaction from the male lead of a storyline" (the term itself comes from a *Green Lantern* story line in which the hero discovers his dead girlfriend's body in a refrigerator). Other period dramas do this as well, of course. *Banished* and *Poldark*, for example, also feature rape narratives which are about masculinity and struggles between men, rather than focusing on their victims. As noted in chapter 1, Ross Poldark uses rape to try to stop Elizabeth from marrying his archenemy Warleggan, and when she does so, George brags that he is "in possession of the field." Her body has become the site of their larger rivalry over land, politics, and banking, rather than important for its own sake. Similarly, in *Banished*, there is a struggle between Major Ross and his junior officer MacDonald over the "loan" of prisoner Kitty McVitie to him, in exchange for MacDonald's promotion. MacDonald tries to set limits on what Kitty can do with the Major: they may "fuck," he tells her, but not share the intimacy of conversation, because it is his masculinity, not Kitty's emotional or physical well-being, that is at stake for him. And so, what Cuklanz described three decades ago regarding rape narratives in popular television remains very much alive in recent costume dramas. Whatever we call it, by prioritizing Mr. Bates's reaction and thirst for revenge, *Downton Abbey*, like the other series this chapter covers later, denies Anna the right to be the center of her own story.

"BUT IT HAPPENED TO *ME*": RAPE IN *A PLACE TO CALL HOME*

The rivalry between men for control of a woman's body and the "loser's" feelings of emasculation plays out in *A Place to Call Home* (APTCH) as well. Though set in the 1950s, this series has been marketed as "the Australian *Downton Abbey*" (2013–2018) and hailed for its "strong" female characters, with an emphasis on their independence and work before and after marriage. Two of the series' story arcs involve rape (Sarah Adams's experiences of rape at Ravensbruck is discussed in chapter 4), and despite the show's feminist credentials, the plots that surround these rapes are much more about the male characters as the actual victims.

When we first meet George's sister, Carolyn (Sara Wiseman), we are quickly made aware that she is the black sheep of the wealthy Bligh family. In her mid-30s, she lives what her mother considers a "Bohemian" lifestyle in the big city (replete with modern art and gay friends who visit her Sydney apartment). When she is reunited with her first love, the small-town doctor Jack Duncan (Craig Hall), she considers settling down to a quiet, domestic life, but before she accepts Jack's marriage proposal, she is raped by her employer, the Harvey Weinstein-esque, powerful newspaper baron, Sir Richard Bennett (Mark Lee), in what viewers would likely recognize as workplace-based "acquaintance rape" made possible by the male exploitation of a woman's desire to progress in her career.

Significantly, the rape itself occupies only a small part of an episode otherwise largely dedicated to exploring issues around masculinity: George is struggling with his memories of his father and debates about what kind of man he has become; his son James is conflicted about his wife's adultery and his homosexuality and future; and Sarah's first husband, Rene, is about to undergo a brain operation in the hope of restoring him to "the man he once was" (episode 3:7). It hence feels inevitable that Carolyn's rape will also be represented in these terms. As though anticipating what is to come, Jack has already warned Carolyn of the dangers of "underestimating" Sir Richard, implying that she is naive to expect equal treatment in the workplace from a—especially an older—man. Jack knows all too well that her employer is "old-fashioned" and not as interested in her work as he is in her body. Nonetheless, Carolyn thinks she can "handle him" and they spend the evening at her apartment, she eager to get his feedback on her article, he pushing alcohol to get her drunk. Jack turns up, realizes that they are drinking together, and, angrily, tells her that she "had promised to be careful": the implication is that by having a drink with a man at home, she is endangering herself. He is soon proved right, and her confidence misplaced, when Sir Richard hits her, and then straddles her on the couch; as we hear her struggling the scene fades out. The next day, Carolyn conceals her bruises and then confronts Sir Richard at work, who tells her no one will believe her given her "history" with men. Carolyn almost accepts his version of events, but when she finally tells Jack, admitting that she has had "lots of men" in the past, she adds that those were "*by my choice* and now one forced himself on me, using every man who came before to justify it . . . he's made me feel cheap and disgusting and unworthy." In this crucial moment, the series foregrounds "a core conviction of feminist theory that women have a *right* of autonomy over their *own* bodies" (Taylor 2016: 341, emphases added).

In this way, the story also critiques cultural attitudes about rape that persist well beyond the 1950s setting of the series: the common use of a woman's sexual history as a defense for rape. Carolyn assumes she cannot seek legal recourse as her reputation would be used against her in court (and a scandal would ruin her brother George's political career), so Jack's violent solution is the closest she will come to any form of justice. Actress Sara Wiseman, in the role of Carolyn, echoed *Downton*'s Joanne Froggatt's assertion that the rape story line in *APTCH*, which aired in 2015, performs a public service: "I really wanted the writers to honor and respect the millions of women that could be watching this and be affected by seeing their lives brought to life on screen" (quoted in Harvey 2017). She also insisted, "It was important for me that it wasn't just brushed over or resolved quickly as it can't be for so many women (who are attacked in real life)." And, indeed, the viewer sees Carolyn drinking heavily and avoiding intimacy with Jack for several episodes after the rape, and the fallout from it continues well into the next series. Nonetheless, the person ultimately less able to get over what has happened is Jack who, like Mr. Bates, can't help but feel "gutted" by his fiancée's rape and fantasizes about seeing Sir Richard "on his knees begging for mercy" (episode 4:8). Also, like Mr. Bates, of course, Jack has his own insecurities which fuel his need for violent revenge. Formerly a POW tortured during World War II, Jack now takes testosterone, so when he decides to teach Carolyn's rapist a lesson, he tells her, "The Japs took my balls once, I'm not losing them a second time." Even when she reminds Jack, "But it happened to *me*!," he replies, "And what happened to *me* is I turned into a gutless coward who won't defend the woman he loves . . . man to man is the only thing that will put an end to it." "It" in this context is clearly Jack's inadequacy, not Carolyn's psychological trauma: when asked if a plan for revenge will help her recovery, she acknowledges only that it will be beneficial for her husband's. She then watches from a distance as Jack challenges Sir Richard to that oldest of masculine clichés, a bare knuckle fight (See figure 2.2), and they wrestle surrounded by a circle of male friends who make sure he can't get away (an interesting twist on the role of complicit bystanders). When Jack at last stands battered but victorious over the bloodied, prostrate body of Sir Richard, Carolyn holds out her arms, and soothingly tells him, "I understand." The audience "understands" all too well: her trauma has been pushed aside by this struggle between men, and her focus, like that of the whole episode, is on the physical and emotional consequences of the plotline for Jack. And this theme continues off-screen too: in interviews for Australian media, Sara Wiseman was asked how such scenes impacted her relationship with her off-screen husband, Craig Hall, who also happens to play Jack (Harvey 2017)—yet again, putting the focus on how a *man* is coping with rape, even though in this case the crime is imaginary.

CAMPUS RAPE AND *KU'DAMM 56* (*BERLIN DANCE SCHOOL 1956*)

Disturbing though it may be to offer male revenge as the best or only justice that can be meted out after rape, *Ku'damm 56* (*Berlin Dance School 1956* (2016)) goes one step further, by suggesting that falling in love with one's rapist is an acceptable way of recovering from the crime. This drama, which was heralded as "Germany's answer to *Mad Men*," is for the most part a nuanced, understated, and stylish bildungsroman which explores the lives of three sisters coming of age in postwar Berlin. Mental illness, homophobia, anti-Semitism, and the legacy of Nazism are handled with sensitivity throughout, but the series' blind spot, as with that of so many other shows we have explored here, is its ill-judged rape plotline. The innocent and unhappy

Figure 2.2 Jack Avenges Carolyn's Rape in *A Place to Call Home*, Episode 4:8 (2015).
Source: Screen grab by Julie Anne Taddeo.

central character, Monika (Sonja Gerhardt), is quietly raped after a party by Joachim (Sabin Tambreu), a wealthy, drunk young man whose privilege makes him think he can take whatever he wants. The rape itself, which takes place in the first episode, feels realistic and appropriately gritty: it is only its aftermath, later in the series, which becomes deeply problematic.

Although the show is set, like *APTCH*, in the 1950s, the rape of a teenager by someone socially successful, and hence with deniability, feels very familiar to contemporary viewers, being evocative of the so-called campus rape we now hear about every day (and Monika's parlor, where the rape occurs, is part of her mother's dance school). Twenty-first-century young women endure, in their schools and university campuses, a rape culture the extent of which is only recently being begun to be reported and understood.[1] Like the rape narratives told in real life by many such young women, Monika does initially seem to be attracted to Joachim, and wishes to impress him, but their actual encounter reveals how quickly her romantic fantasy can turn into a nightmare. He gets unattractively drunk at her sister's wedding and is asleep and snoring by the time she brings him coffee: he then gets her name wrong, making it clear that all girls are interchangeable and the same to him. As the scene unfolds, he becomes increasingly aggressive, and then grabs her around the throat while he rapes her. Joachim epitomizes the problems of twenty-first-century rape culture in young men, as indicated by his disregard of consent and dismissal of all women as merely sex objects, telling Monika that "no woman [wants to] but they do it anyway." Even more dangerous is his choking hold around her throat, which has recently become infamous as a crossover from violent pornography that has killed many (especially young) women in real life and yet has been frequently defended in court as a "sex game gone wrong" (Moore and Khan 2019: in the UK this defense is the subject of an influential campaign, We Can't Consent to This, which looks likely to change the law around "rough sex"). In this way, many of the issues our society faces are brought together by this scene, and the camera stresses Monika's shock and distress by focusing on her horrified face throughout, and then panning to the stain on the ceiling above which represents her now tarnished life.

The viewer knows this is a "real rape," but unlike Anna in *Downton*, Monika's account is not believed by others. Because her attacker is very attractive, and popular with women, no one takes him at all seriously as a perpetrator (a similar narrative pattern takes place in the aforementioned *Promising Young Woman*, and the link with many reports of real-life campus rape are clear). Afterward, her rather monstrous mother sees the attack as an opportunity to bring about a socially advantageous marriage between the two but cannot argue with, and indeed half-believes, Joachim when he states it was consensual and that Monika is a "slut" (episode 2). Then Monika's suffering is compounded by social pressure when she is later made to go on a date with him, at which point even her initially sympathetic sisters soon decide that she is lucky to have the attentions of someone so handsome and rich. Monika brings a knife along with her on the date, however, and the viewer expects, and probably hopes, that the series will develop into a rape-revenge plot. She does indeed stab Joachim in his side, but the wound is only a superficial one, and from this point on her rage and fear begins to abate and the show begins the process of turning her rapist into a romantic hero. The viewer is now invited to feel sorry for the tortured Joachim, who like Monika is struggling to find his place in the world and who shares with her a problematic and damaging relationship with his parent. His casual cruelty toward women is meant to be excused by this back story and his misogyny stems from lack of self-worth—which the love of a good woman (whom he decides is Monika) can correct. By the end of the series, Monika has redeemed him without even trying: he is in love with and wants to marry her even though she has become pregnant with another man's child. This is the only revenge Monika is able to achieve in the show, for she plans, at her mother's suggestion, to trick him into marriage by pretending the child is his—the "only weapon we women have" as her mother says. Once she confesses, however, the show implies that her brief deception means she and Joachim are now equal in damaging misbehavior and can start afresh. They signal this forgiveness and equilibrium by having passionate consensual sex, and although Monika turns down his marriage proposal at the end of season 1, it is more to do with her desire to travel and dance than the rape itself—and they do then marry in the finale of season 2 (set three years later) of *Ku'damm 59* (2018).

This "falling in love with one's rapist" plotline echoes that which we explored in *Banished* in chapter 1, but it seems more surprising here given, unlike *Banished*, the rape itself is not at all romantic and there is no question of pleasure for the victim. It is only by a determined focus on Joachim as male lead that his redemption and their eventual reconciliation seem possible and even desirable. Perhaps even more disturbing, however, is the way the rape sets in motion a process of transformation for Monika. She slowly becomes a different person over the course of season 1: following the rape, she begins to rebel against her domineering mother, searches for the truth about her father, starts a blossoming career as a dancer, and has an enjoyable "friends-with-benefits" affair with her dance partner. In this regard, the long-term damage inflicted by such a crime is downplayed. Far from ruining her life, her rape is represented as an upsetting but probably inevitable rite of passage for a girl growing up, which becomes the catalyst for her to break free from what has been up to this point a limited and repressed existence. Indeed, it marks the moment when she leaves behind old prewar values and embraces modernity and youth culture, as signified by the rock 'n' roll music which provides the soundtrack to the series and which she grows to love.

As Read has argued, this idea of the victim undergoing a positive transformation following an attack is a common trope in rape-revenge film, often representing a movement toward a more independent, physically and mentally tough heroine, and we can certainly see those ideas at work here (e.g., Monika's sister comments on how strong she has become: "You have muscles everywhere!," she says). However, in the characters Read explores—like Catwoman in *Batman Returns* or Julia Roberts's victim of spousal abuse in *Sleeping with the Enemy*—the transformation is into a powerful vigilante figure who finally avenges herself upon her rapist. In this show, the process only transforms Monika into the kind of woman—sexy, free, fun, and athletic, essentially a type of Manic Pixie Dream Girl—Joachim or any man would wish to marry (Rabin, 2010).

Ku'damm 56's mutation of the rape-revenge plot into a romance seems deeply problematic in a number of ways, then. And with this in mind, it is all the more surprising that, along with several of the other shows we explore here, the audience not only accepted the way the rape plot ends up but encouraged it to happen. In chapter 1, we speculated that distance from the wild and lawless eighteenth century made rape fantasy and post-rape "shipping" possible in *Banished* and *Poldark*, but, with an urban setting and focus on music and cars, this is a much more recognizably modern show, and it is hard not to find it uncomfortably close to home. Yet, though aired in 2016–2018, on the eve of and post-#MeToo (and internationally on Netflix in 2020), fans did not express concern over the rape nor did they need the distance of centuries to fantasize about romance for its two leads, as the showrunner, Annette Hess, was noted to observe in a newspaper interview:

> Hess says she enjoyed hearing from viewers who were willing Monika and potential love interest Joachim to marry. Monika rejected Joachim in *Ku'damm 56* but he returns in the sequel. . . . "There are a lot of fans asking for marriage and happy endings between him and Monika so it's wonderful to see all these Facebook posts," the writer says. "It's quite new that the writer has direct reaction to what you have written. They said after the first part it has to go on, they have to marry and I'm giving the fans this marriage but not in the way they are expecting." (Pickard, 2018)

There is no sense, from in this interview and clearly among the fan base for this show, that loving marriage to one's rapist is an inappropriate story line. Admittedly, the first series, which features the rape and initially charters Joachim's redemption, is pre-#MeToo, but both this interview and the most recent series, in which he marries his former victim, is not—and is thus surprising to see on our screens in 2019. Clearly, fans and journalists, as well as writers and showrunners, are prepared to turn a blind eye to the horrors of rape. This disturbing reality—that our society as a whole is complicit in rape culture—is both displayed by and critiqued in *Outlander*, the subject of our final case study below.

OUTLANDER AND COLLECTIVE COMPLICITY

Justice for rape victims never occurs in the courtroom in eighteenth-century set *Outlander* any more than it does in any of the shows explored here: this is a space which remains curiously absent for victims of sexual assault in so many of these period dramas. But 2019's season 4 presented writers and showrunners with a new dilemma as they adapted Gabaldon's later novels in which the rape of Jamie and Claire's daughter Brianna (aka "Bree," played by Sophie Skelton), who travels from 1960s Boston to 1770s North Carolina to find her parents, is essential to all that follows. Critics were watchful to see how recent events would influence the series moving forward: "Because of Time's Up and Me Too, *Outlander* may finally have to deal with its rape problem"—as one blogger put it (Weekes 2018). Executive producer, Maril Davis, added, "We're sensitive to what's going on in this time right now" (quoted in Weiss 2018).

As a result, the way the rape is screened is notably different from previous ones in *Outlander* and, in particular, in stark contrast with the explicit, detailed assault on Jamie at the end of season 1. Starz network issued a pre-transmission warning that the episode included "a portrayal of sexual violence" and shared the phone number for the National Sexual Assault Hotline at the end (which it had not done for previous *Outlander* rapes). Moreover, and unusually for most of the dramas we explore here, there is no gratuitous graphic rape scene: the actual rape takes place off camera. The show in fact makes a clear visual distinction between sex and rape, for immediately prior to her assault, we witness instead a very lengthy and consensual sex scene between Brianna and her newly betrothed, Roger Wakefield (Richard Rankin). It is fine to gain pleasure from viewing loving sex, the drama makes clear, but no longer from viewing rape.

In the scene in question, Brianna (postcoitally arguing with Roger) returns to the tavern where she is staying; there she encounters the pirate Stephen Bonnet (Ed Speleers) and follows him into the backroom to negotiate over her mother's wedding band, which he had stolen from Claire in a previous episode. Once alone together, he strikes and drags her across the floor before he shuts and locks the door, but the camera then focuses on the customers and staff on the other side of the door, who smirk, continuing their drinking and card game while she cries for help off-screen. This represents a significant change in setting from the novel itself, as in the source text this rape has no witnesses. Hence this rewriting of the original becomes a powerful statement clearly in dialogue with #MeToo. The camera's focus on the bystanders reminds the viewer of the complicity of those who turn a blind eye to sexual violence, with echoes of the Harvey Weinstein and Jeffrey Epstein revelations of the paid employees who enabled acts of sexual assault by powerful men (Schultz, 2018). As one fan on Twitter expressed about *Outlander*, "The rape scene is SO much more chilling because while we hear Brianna's screams, we see that NO ONE is going to help her" (December 23, 2018). Here *Outlander* acknowledges that rape is not solely about the victim and the perpetrator but also about the culture which allows or condones it.

Yet while *Outlander*'s fourth season does give the sense of positive changing attitudes toward sexual violence in our culture, in other ways it reminds us how little these plotlines have changed. As previously noted, recourse to the courts is never an option in *Outlander*, so much so that when Brianna suggests pressing charges, she is told by a male friend it would only bring her more shame. Moreover, while in the short term the drama is completely sympathetic to Brianna (showing us her bruised back and bloodied undergarments as she bathes at the basin after the rape, wincing in pain, followed in the next episode by her nightmares), over the whole of series 4 that consideration of the victim becomes secondary to other issues, as we saw in *Downton*. She becomes pregnant, so questions of the child's parentage, Jamie's need to avenge his daughter's "honor," and Roger's struggle to accept a child that may not be his are instead paramount. What Brianna's rape then provides is yet another adventure for Jamie and even a chance at redemption for her rapist Bonnet, who, when later forgiven by Brianna, makes what he sees as a magnanimous gesture: pulling a ruby from his mouth, he gives it to her "for [the] maintenance of the child," he says.

So far, we can see similarities with *Downton*'s rape, but shockingly, fan responses also suggested that a romance plotline like that in *Ku'damm 56* would be eagerly received by viewers. As one fan, praising Ed Speleers's performance, noted at the time,

> I think way way down the road there could be redemption and even romance [between the rapist and his victim] . . . the way Ed Speleers plays Bonnet I can't help but find myself wanting to see so much more of this character. (Youtube, 2019)

Perhaps part of the problem here is that Bonnet is played by the same actor as *Downton Abbey*'s handsome servant Jimmy, while Roger, like Claire's twentieth-century husband Frank (Tobias Menzies), is an academic—who in *Outlander*'s eighteenth-century world of muscular kilted men and sexy pirates seems sorely out of place.

Fortunately, the following episodes make it clear that Bree will *not* follow in the footsteps of Monika in *Ku'damm 56* and fall in love with Bonnet, despite his good looks. He will, however, continue to torment Roger, who finds the ruby hidden among his wife's things in season 5. Roger confronts Bree, perhaps doubting the truth of her story about the encounter as a rape and again struggling with the ambiguity of their child's parentage. Male anxiety once again takes precedence over the rape of the loved one: when they have sex, for example, Roger needs reassurance that Bree "enjoyed herself" to restore his confidence in his masculinity (just as Anna's pregnancy in *Downton*'s final season functions to restore Mr. Bates's manhood).

And, as always, revenge is carried out by men. In the aftermath of Brianna's rape, it is Jamie who must first be protected, since Claire fears he will feel guilty for having previously rescued Bonnet from the gallows for a different crime, and then once he knows, Jamie naturally seeks revenge, mistakenly beating Roger for his daughter's rape, then hunting for Bonnet, and so on. Later, Roger too nearly beats Bonnet to death. Bree intervenes and insists Bonnet be tried in court, where he is sentenced to death. This is probably not for rape, however: we don't see the actual trial, but the sentence seems to be for his other crimes, namely piracy, smuggling, and kidnapping, as though rape alone is not enough to merit proper punishment. And while some kind of female rape-revenge plot *is* invoked when Bonnet, awaiting death by drowning, is shot in the head by Bree, this feels like "rape-revenge-lite." Bree's motive remains unclear to the viewer and may be more an act of mercy than revenge, given Bonnet had confided to her his terror of dying at sea. Similarly, the leader of the gang who rapes Claire in season 5 (discussed in more detail in chapter 7) is killed by Claire's stepdaughter, Marsali—but only after most of the gang have been already violently punished by Jamie and his clan. Claire herself, due to her vows only to save life, refuses to avenge her rape, terrible though it has been. The show cannot, it seems, conceive of an unapologetically vengeful heroine: real revenge seems to be men's work.

CONCLUSION

There is no revenge, violent or otherwise, which can cure a rape survivor of her trauma and atone for the horror of her experience. In the past, films which implied that it could, and followed the victim's desire for vengeance, were often reductive or exploitative in nature. But recent examples of rape-revenge, like *Promising Young Woman*, do remind us that women have a right to be angry and that we, the audience, should be angry too on their behalf. The law may still fail to punish rape, but the powerful heroines of these kinds of stories will hand out their own retribution, and in this fantasy of revenge there is some satisfaction to be had. Period drama on the small screen, however, by and large denies women this rage. Its survivors are sad and traumatized, yes, but not vengeful. They must recover from their pain rather than inflict it on another. Instead, their lovers and husbands seek retribution on their behalf, and in doing so change the focus of the narrative. Rape thus risks being reduced to a plot device which furthers the development of a male character—even when that character is also the rapist, as in the case of *Ku'damm 56*.

It is significant that none of these dramas ever give us formal, legal justice for the victim of rape. In real life, cases of rape in the eighteenth- and twentieth-century worlds of *Outlander* and *Downton Abbey* or *APTCH* did sometimes make it to the courts and even sometimes resulted in punishments (albeit minor ones) for the perpetrator, especially if the victim was upper class. The characters in these shows have no confidence in the law to help them, though, and choose to seek a much older form of justice. Such plots may make us reflect on how little progress society has made in this regard: as these characters reject the legal systems of years past, the viewer is reminded of the continuing inadequacies of rape prosecution today. The problem with the vengeance depicted in these shows, however, is that it seems to construct rape as a "personal" matter, one to be sorted out among men, between families, and behind closed doors, rather than a problem for the whole of society to deal with. Such revenge plots not only sideline the female victim but also ignore the need for the legal and institutional reform which would make rape properly punishable and make violent revenge unnecessary. It might be satisfying for viewers to see villains on screen get what they deserve—but it ignores the fact that for the majority of modern survivors of rape, there is no justice at all, by fists or any other means.

NOTE

1. See, for example, Meredith Minister (2018), *Rape Culture on Campus* (Lanham, MD: Lexington Books); but sexual assault of girls and women at school and university isn't specific to the United States, as a 2020 report, in chapter 1, *Sexual Assault in Australia*, detailed that the sexual assault rate was higher for those aged fifteen to nineteen (455 assaults per 100,000) than any other age group. Overall, the rate of sexual assaults reported to police was seven times higher for women compared with men (https://www.theguardian.com/australia-news/2020/aug/28/australian-women-in-their-late-teens-more-likely-to-be-victims-of-sexual-assault).

Chapter 3

"Dismissed, Ignored, and Woefully Underreported"

Male Rape in Bridgerton *and* Outlander

Male rape remains a "forgotten history" (Javaid 2016). Brownmiller's influential *Against Our Will*, for example, contains hardly any reference to the rape of men—except, memorably and controversially, to say she wished to see men raped in film instead of always assaults on women (1975: 303). Through history, male rape was associated with institutions, namely prisons, and with gay men: it was not thought to be a real issue outside of these communities until the 1980s. Hence it only became illegal to rape a man in Britain after the Criminal Justice and Public Order Act in 1994, and even after this point, the crime remained chronically underreported and largely unacknowledged by the public:

> The notion of male rape is overlooked because of the strong gender stereotypes into which men and women are socialised. Men have traditionally been expected to be strong and dominant and this expectation disallows them to be victims of a sexual offence which fundamentally threatens their sexuality and manliness. (Abdullah-Khan, 2008: 6)

Of course, shame and guilt have always haunted female victims of rape too, but as we have discussed elsewhere in this book, the discourse around it did begin to change after the feminist movement of the 1970s. Feminism, which did so much to seek justice for female survivors, has, however, been regarded as problematic for male rape victims. "At the crux of the feminist position is the identification of males as the perpetrators of rape and women as their victims . . . as such, feminist work has ignored the fact that men too are raped" (Abdullah-Khan, 2008: 69). Feminist frameworks remain the most helpful way of exploring the problem rape posits in our society but as they have constructed it as primarily a male crime against women, they have not provided a way of examining it as a crime against men—indeed arguably closing down those conversations. Of course, approximately 90 percent of rape victims *are* women, but that means that huge numbers of men have also been raped—approximately around 3 percent of American men, for example (RAINN 2020). It is only in the past decade that scholarship like that quoted in this chapter has started to give a voice to the survivors of male rape. And, even more than female victims, male rape survivors are likely to encounter disbelief or derision when they report their victimization. In addition, male victims, both straight and gay, face the added risk of homophobia (Capers 2011).

Given this, it is unsurprising, then, that on television and in film, male rape has been mostly relegated to prison dramas like *Oz* (1997–2003) and *The Shawshank Redemption* (1994). As Bennett Capers (2011) observes, we, as a society, tend to regard male prisons as "zones without laws" where rape is simply an additional punishment for one's crimes, and so such scenes of male on male sexual violence on TV or film are par for the course. As Claire Cohen has discussed, TV comedy also contains a number of passing references to male sexual assault, but with a disturbing tendency to dismiss them and play them for laughs (2014: 79–87). More recently, however, this has been expanded to other, more serious depictions of toxic masculinity. Teen dramas like Netflix's *13 Reasons Why* (2017–2020) have incorporated "ripped from the headlines" stories about the sexually violent teen male locker room. And the extent to which popular culture has started to acknowledge male rape is reflected by, or even as a result of, its recent inclusion in British soap opera and the resulting tabloid coverage of these plotlines.

It was initially the rape of a gay character in the long-running British soap opera *Hollyoaks* (1995–) which provided the "first step" for mainstream television to examine the subject. According to Duncan Craig, from the organization Survivors Manchester, this first male rape plotline in 2000 prepared a television audience for the, it seems, even more shocking, 2018 rape of a straight, male, long-standing, and popular character David Platt, in *Coronation Street* (McGraph 2018). Craig was a consultant on both shows and hoped that these plotlines—which aired eighteen years apart from each other—would reach real-life victims of the crime:

> "It's two very different audiences and characters," he says. "John Paul is a gay man, David is a straight man, so we're tackling masculinity in a very different way. . . . Maybe, without 'Hollyoaks' doing the John Paul storyline, we wouldn't be able to have the 'Coronation Street' story. . . . I want [the audience] to try their hardest to understand what it's like as a male survivor and what it's like to see things on television that are exaggerated and how that makes them feel. . . . My priority is the man that's sat at home watching this on the television,

or listening to the radio, who is a silent survivor. I need to make sure he understands that there is help and support out there."(Quoted in McGraph 2018)

Craig achieved his aim: male rape crisis helplines like the national charity *Male Survivors* received a huge increase in calls after *Coronation Street*'s episode aired (BBC News 2018), reminding us how much television plotlines matter in real life. Nonetheless, the broadcast was shocking for many viewers, resulting in over 100 complaints being made to Ofcom (the British regulatory body for communication of all kinds) (Rackham 2018). As is apparent by the many examples in this book, female rape is both more mainstream and somehow more palatable to watch: the rape of an eighteen-year-old girl in *Coronation Street* in a 2020 episode, for example, did not provoke at all the same outrage as the Platt story line did.

Nonetheless, there is a sense in which it is now becoming more commonplace to see male rape on screen, and a wider understanding of what rape is and the many forms it can take. For example, Michaela Coel's critically acclaimed *I May Destroy You* (BBC, 2020) featured another scene which its actors identified as "a historical moment in British TV" (Power 2020): a rape which occurs immediately after consensual sex between two gay men who have just hooked up on Grindr. Kwame (Paapa Essiedu), one of the central characters in the show, is traumatized by the attack but initially unsure that what has just happened to him actually constitutes rape; it is only after visiting the police station to talk about Arabella's (Michaela Coel) assault that he realizes this attack also "counts." Despite this, however, the *straight* policeman who takes his statement is by turns incredulous and unsupportive, and hence Kwame withdraws his complaint. The contrast with Arabella's much more positive experience of the justice system is marked, reminding the viewer that our society's understanding of male rape has a long way to go—especially when the victim is gay. And this "withdrawal of consent after consent" plotline is just one of the ways in which *I May Destroy You* pulls apart society's long-held views about rape. Arabella also experiences, from someone she considers her boyfriend, the less-discussed sexual violence that is "stealthing" (the act of nonconsensual condom removal), another version of which we will explore further in the next section.

MALE RAPE BY WOMEN: *BRIDGERTON* AND *OUTLANDER*

As this book has demonstrated, the rape of women has been a staple in period drama for decades, typically justified with the pat explanation that rape adds "authenticity" to historical fiction. But #MeToo has made viewers, and as a result, TV writers adapting source material, more sensitive to how consent is portrayed on our screens when it applies to male victims as well as female and, as we have indicated earlier, more aware of the different ways in which men can be raped. That said, those representations are not without their issues. One of the most talked about period drama hits of recent years, Netflix's Georgian-set *Bridgerton* (2020–), features a problematic sex act between its two leads. This series is adapted from Julia Quinn's 2000 historical romance novel *The Duke and I* and contained a scene which even many of its pre-#MeToo readers interpreted as male rape. Newly wed but sexually ignorant Daphne finally realizes that when Simon, the Duke of Hastings, tells her, "I can't have children," what he really means is "I won't" and that he achieves this by the (never reliable) withdrawal method. In the book, angry over the deception, she takes advantage of him while he is asleep:

> She felt the strangest, most intoxicating surge of power. He was in her control, she realized. He was asleep, and probably still more than a little bit drunk, and she could do whatever she wanted with him. She could have whatever she wanted. . . . She held him to her while he poured his seed into her. (Quinn 2000: 337–338)

In the 2020 TV adaptation, Simon (Regé-Jean Page) is neither drunk nor asleep when his wife (played by Phoebe Dynevor) takes her revenge, having been planning it for some time. Indeed, he is initially pleased over the unusual sexual assertiveness she shows, taking off her clothes, rolling on top of him, and pinning him to the bed with her thighs. Eager to avoid ejaculation and hence pregnancy, however, he says, "Wait, wait," but Daphne keeps going, and he cannot stop her until it is too late. Their marriage immediately degenerates into rage and recrimination, but, disturbingly for many viewers, the emphasis and the plotlines that follow are mostly focused on Simon's treatment of Daphne, rather than hers of him. Simon is initially angry and outraged by what we might describe as a female version of stealthing but soon seems to accept his wife's belief that, by lying to her and taking advantage of her sexual innocence, the real betrayal of consent was his. As Aja Romano argues,

> The strangest thing about this moment is that I'm not sure the show's writers consider this scene to be a rape scene . . . depriving Simon of his consent to both sex and fatherhood, even at the moment of climax, is still rape. (2020)

Certainly, the way the whole scene is filmed eroticizes the incident: Daphne is, unusually for their sex scenes, completely naked, and the camera lingers on Simon's face and body and emphasizes his pleasure prior to the crucial moment. More problematic still, the casting of the show meant that, as one Twitter post noted angrily, it was "a white woman raping a Black man. Sooooooo. Fuck that shit" (joie@morebookstofind 25 Dec 2020) and then, as Romano adds, immediately making it his fault:

> This makes it even more egregious that the show is glossing over the incident. Men are often considered silent victims of sexual assault, and Black men in particular are often made scapegoats for sexual violence, which further erases the status of Black male victims of sexual assault. In this context, the show's emphasis on Simon as the instigator of Daphne's choice basically paints him as being responsible for his own rape. This aligns with the broader cultural gaslighting of Black men and the shifting of blame away from the white men and women who enact violence upon them. (Romano, 2020)[1]

One of the most interesting aspects of *Bridgerton* is its replacement of the usually entirely white aristocracy of the past with one which has as many black characters, something probably unique for a period drama, but its politics are much less sensitive when it comes to this plotline. *Bridgerton* takes very seriously the attempted rape of Daphne by a drunken, rejected suitor in episode 2: Lord Berbrooke's attack on her, though swiftly rebuffed when she punches him, is readily accepted by her family as more than enough grounds for his disgrace. The series cannot, it seems, show the same narrative care toward Simon's. Indeed, its treatment of this subject matter reflects a still-persisting belief about male consent: that men cannot, really, be raped by women. This is a belief upheld in law: still the main legislation on rape in the UK, The Sexual Offences Act of 2003, states that rape occurs when a person "intentionally penetrates the vagina, anus or mouth of another person (B) with his penis, B does not consent to the penetration, and (c)A does not reasonably believe that B consents." As Claire Cohen notes, this implies that a woman cannot commit the crime: she can only be found guilty of a lesser offense. The Stern Review (2010) report unwittingly reinforced this idea; the emphasis on penetration by a penis undermines the seriousness of crimes against men and perpetuates the idea that if men are physically capable of a sex act, it is not a crime. In this regard, *Bridgerton*'s refusal to take Simon's withdrawal of consent seriously is symptomatic of a wider social issue.

This is further reflected in *Outlander*, perhaps the show most preoccupied with male rape—we explore three of them in this chapter—but one which also seems to have a much more cavalier attitude to consent when a beautiful woman is the perpetrator. For example, in the 2017 episode, "Of Lost Things" (screened just days before #MeToo was first used as a hashtag by Alyssa Milano), the central character Jamie Fraser (Sam Heughan) is essentially blackmailed into sleeping with Lady Geneva Dunsany (Hannah James) when she threatens to expose his true Jacobite rebel identity to her British family. As originally written by Diana Gabaldon in 1993, what started as coerced sex on Geneva's part suddenly turned into rape on Jamie's, as executive producer Maril Davis explained,

> In the book, there's a question of whether or not Jamie rapes Geneva, because he does say, "When I start I won't be able to stop." And she does at one point say, "No, no." And he continues. We decided not to include that part, merely because that's not what the scene is about. The scene is about Jamie taking comfort in someone that he doesn't love. But he feels empathy for this character even though he's coerced into Geneva's bed, he still feels like he wants, as a gentleman, for it to be a satisfying or non-threatening experience for her. (Davis quoted in Napoli 2017)

Critics therefore embraced this TV rewrite as a positive step to "fix the 1993 novel's consent issue" (Sarner 2017), and we might also note that, after two seasons in which fans followed Jamie's trauma and recovery from his own rape by Black Jack Randall, it would, perhaps, be too much to ask them to witness Jamie commit a similar act upon another. Indeed, this difference goes to the heart of the process of adapting *Outlander* for the screen, for, like *Bridgerton*, the source texts (this time written in the 1990s) have less sensitivity toward the representation of rape than we expect today:

> That's what's truly fascinating about *Outlander*. The real temporal displacement it must negotiate is not the two centuries between Jamie and Claire, but rather the changing cultural conversation around consent in the decades between the books and the show. (Sarner 2017)

The makers of *Outlander* have to constantly bear this issue in mind when weighing up fidelity to the source text with the changing expectation of a post-#MeToo audience. But Davis's explanation ignores that in both Gabaldon's and the 2017 TV version of this scene, the encounter, as arranged, is itself an act of sexual coercion, with Jamie, a prisoner employed in Lady Geneva's household, himself a victim. In episode 11 of season 5, the writers further remove any negative association with this bedroom scene, when Jamie tells his daughter Brianna, "It wasn't a matter of love between us, but it was our choice . . . and that's all I'll say about it." In fact, Jamie had no "choice" if he wanted to stay out of prison, and by romanticizing this encounter, *Outlander* is fundamentally reinforcing old rape fantasy myths like those we explore in chapter 1 in relation to *Banished* and *Poldark*. Indeed, given that this coerced sex results in the death of Geneva while giving birth to Jamie's illegitimate son William, the whole plotline can be considered a kind of rewriting of the "ravishment," pregnancy, and death of Elizabeth in *Poldark*. Unlike Elizabeth, however, Jamie—and presumably the intended viewer—does not seem to regret what has happened in the long term, so wholeheartedly has this series reversed his initial disgust and rage. The audience is reassured that coerced sex by a younger woman cannot really be rape—and of course, Jamie has already survived something the series represents as much more serious and damaging: rape by a man—as our next section will discuss. The very idea that a man could be raped by a woman is still used in other period dramas for comedic effect. In the Spanish period soap opera *Velvet Colección* (2018), for example, the department store employee Manuel visits the compound of Patty Samira, a charlatan guru with a penchant for handsome young men. After unwittingly taking a hallucinogen, he awakens the next day, naked, and unable to recall anything that happened. When he tells his male coworkers about his evening, which clearly involved an act of nonconsensual sex, they treat it as a joke (after all Patty is an attractive woman, he should be glad, they imply), and he quickly forgets about it.

One of the fascinating things about *Outlander*, however, is the way it changes in response to the events of #MeToo: by the end of season 3, in an episode screened in December 2017, another rape by a woman is a far from humorous experience and fully recognized as rape (Doyle 2019). The difference in treatment may be, however, because Young Ian (John Bell) is a teenager, raped by an older woman, a witch known as the Bakra/Geillis, who bathes in goat blood and kills male virgins after bedding them as part of a ritual to maintain her youth. This stereotype of the female predator whose main aim is to stay young and beautiful at all costs is a common trope in popular culture, with countless representations dating from the legend of Elizabeth Bathory onward, all with the message that women will do almost anything to preserve their youth. From a purely feminist perspective, then, this plotline is a troubling one. For Jamie earlier in the series, being coerced into sex by a younger, more innocent and highly fertile woman was ultimately a positive experience, whereas nothing could be more terrifying than a sexually predatory, middle-aged woman worried about looking older! And as seems inevitable with rapes by women, the rape is still sexualized, even though sinister: when Ian first sees the Bakra, she is getting out of a bath of blood, in a scene which recalls Ingrid Pitt's famously sexy portrayal of *Countess Dracula* in the Hammer Horror classic (1971). Lotte Verbeek (as Geillis), herself a former model, manages to look both evil and erotic in this scene (the blood resembles red latex on her skin) but, to be fair to *Outlander*, the show does ultimately make clear that Young Ian is terrified of her, rather than—or at least as well as—aroused. Moreover, while we see her begin to caress him, we do not see the rape itself: once she opens her robe, the camera quickly cuts away to the opening credits.

Instead of a gratuitous rape scene, we instead get only the traumatic impact it has had on Ian when he finally tells Jamie about it in a graveyard in the next season (episode 4:1). In this regard, this plot serves an important function, communicating the need to speak about male rape. Jamie, whose recurrent victim status is used in the series to give him credibility as he consoles others who are raped, urges Ian to share his pain in order to heal it: "Some ghosts can only be banished by speaking their name and foul deeds aloud," adding that "I too had a festering pain inside, until I shared it with your Aunt Claire." According to Kilbourne (2019; quoted in Naugle), "Most male rape victims . . . have to be encouraged to come forward, the shame and stigma is so deep," and Jamie knows this only too well, for he has himself to be cajoled by Claire into communication about his own ordeal. ("We've barely even talked about it," she says during a fight, "Tell me, goddamn it. Talk to me, make me understand.") Once Jamie does, the couple takes a major step toward healing, and he is able in turn to better support other survivors. And, in this instance, he serves to educate the audience as much as comfort Ian, for their conversation "debunks a myth about male rape as he explains that it's possible to have an erection and still be raped": "People understand that a man can be anally penetrated. . . . But if he has an erection, they think, Doesn't that mean it was consensual? It's hard for people to imagine" (Kilbourne, quoted in Naugle). When Ian confides that Geillis "made me do unspeakable things," he breaks down, and asks Jamie,

> "Have you ever lain wi' someone when ye didna want to do it?"
> "I have."
> "Then ye understand how it can be—how you can do it without wishing to, detesting it, and all the while, it feels pleasing?"

Trying to ease the tension, Jamie jokes, "What it comes down to is your cock doesn't have the conscience that you have," but the point about male consent is a serious one, and not one often explored in television, which more commonly reinforces the old belief that, as Mika Doyle (2019) notes,

> Men are supposed to be hungry for sex always—so they can't be raped. Men should be strong enough to fight off attackers—so they can't be raped. Both of those myths, rooted in traditional concepts of masculinity, contribute to a culture in which male rape is dismissed, ignored, and woefully underreported.

Ian has been capable of performing a sex act, but it is still unmistakably rape. In this way, this plotline is an important one, by reminding the viewer that women, even beautiful ones, can also be abusers and thus challenging "historical and cultural stereotypes that present women as subordinate and passive, both sexually and physically, along with the idea that men are solely the offenders in sex crimes" (Doyle 2019). That said, however, the most brutal and talked about rape in the show *is* committed by a man, and it is rather more problematic in terms of its gender politics, as we will explore in our next section.

"THE MOST GRAPHIC DEPICTION OF SEXUAL ASSAULT ON TELEVISION": JAMIE'S RAPE BY RANDALL

Actress Caitriona Balfe hoped that all the near-rape encounters her time-traveling character Claire manages to escape in *Outlander*'s first season in 2014–2015 would "spark[s] some kind of a conversation and maybe an awareness" of how rape was "a weapon used against women" and "is still unfortunately, throughout a lot of the world and here (Scotland)" (quoted in Debnath 2015). It is, however, her eighteenth-century husband who actually becomes the victim of rape by the end of the season. But, as noted earlier, with a few exceptions, this genre has shied away from male rape—not just as a weapon of war used against other *men*—thus making *Outlander*'s recurring story line of male rape—and male trauma—unusual and indeed ground breaking. Jamie's rape by "Black" Jack Randall, at the end of the first series, though covered extensively by media outlets at the time of its airing in 2015, is worth revisiting here. The series used Jamie's rape to prioritize male rape as more traumatic for its victims, as much of series 2 focused on Jamie's physical and emotional damage and his long road to recovery. But to its credit, instead of making Jamie's rape an anomaly, the following rape of Fergus, also by Randall, and Ian's assault, by Geillis, performed essential work in raising awareness about the prevalence of male on male (and even female on male, as we have seen) sexual violence.

Outlander's first season ended with what has been described as "the most graphic depiction of [. . .] sexual assault [. . .] on television" (Bonner 2015). A cynical viewer might observe that while female rape on screen is so commonplace as to be quotidian, the rape of a man is rarely seen on television and hence became a major talking point for the show. It must also be acknowledged, however, that *Outlander* was unusual in its portrayal of rape and torture so graphic—and detailed, in scenes lasting for two episodes—as to be rare in period drama or indeed on television more generally. The rape unfolds through a series of flashbacks recalled by the deeply traumatized, suicidal Jamie after the rape and includes a violent anal penetration as well as psychological torture (see Fig 3.1).

Such scenes were, on the whole, sympathetically received by fans: the rape enhanced Heughan's acting reputation, with fans on social media heralding

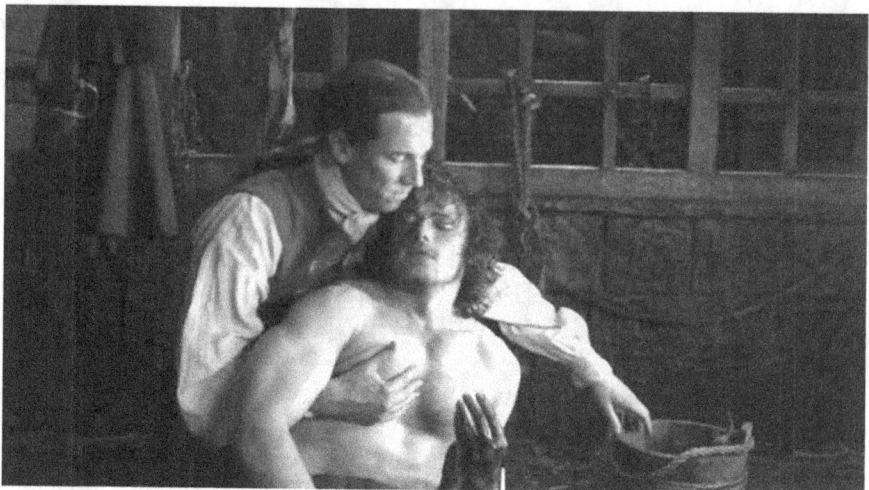

Figure 3.1 "Black" Jack Randall Prepares to Rape Jamie in *Outlander*, Episode 1:16 (2015). *Source*: Screen grab by Julie Anne Taddeo.

his performance as "groundbreaking" and "brave." Critics acknowledged sensitive handling of the material and an avoidance of reductive characters or narrative clichés: the rapist (British officer "Black" Jack Randall, played by handsome actor Tobias Menzies) is presented not as a "monster" but as "a real human being," for example (Blake 2016). Nonetheless, this show is disturbing not only for its explicitness but also for its alignment of the desiring gaze of both the audience and the heroine with Randall, the rapist. Much of the series' enduring appeal has rested on Jamie's (and actor Sam Heughan's) positioning as a "Scottish hunk": like *Poldark*, the show regularly features shots of him semi-naked. However, as Rachel Moseley and Gemma Goodman have observed, "while a desiring gaze is invited and rewarded in *Outlander*, it is also complicated, even compromised" by the camera's lingering on Jamie's perfectly muscled body, initially as a scarred victim of flogging and later as a bruised and battered victim of rape:

> As the narrative progresses, and we gain access in flashback to Jamie's flogging, we become aware that our desiring gaze is shared with "Black" Jack Randall [. . .] the potential for complicity with Claire as the woman who looks with desire at Jamie (and her counterpart the viewer) is made explicit in the final episodes of the first series, [. . .] Jamie, in his semi-conscious, traumatized state, repeatedly confuses Claire with Randall. [. . .] As we see her face merge with Randall's through Jamie's eyes, the gazes of the desiring woman, the audience, and the sadistic representative of the English army align. (Moseley & Goodman, 2018: 65-66)

Outlander is uncomfortable viewing not only because of its sadism but because the viewer is made to feel complicit in the violence unfolding on screen. Explicit rape scenes like this have long been controversial: the most well-known example is probably the ten-minute-long depiction of gang rape in *The Accused* (1988). This film became famous partly for this dramatization of rape, which some critics argued was gratuitous (and problematic as seen through the eyes of a male bystander, not recounted by the heroine), and others believed that was deeply necessary as a scene which brought home to the audience the horrors of the crime.[2] The same could be said of rape in *Outlander*, but this series, which showrunner Ron Moore admitted sets out to "make you look at something uncomfortable and feel it" (quoted in Prudom 2013), asks especially difficult questions of its audience about their viewing pleasure. This is particularly problematic in the final rape scene, which some viewers *have* described as "pornographic" because even though it is certainly not consensual it involves some sexual pleasure for the victim and perhaps also for the viewer (Prudom). It could be argued that this is another version of the rape fantasy we have discussed in chapter 1 on *Poldark* and *Banished*, but given the violence which has gone before, not one which any viewer can be comfortable with.

This tendency to eroticize male rape for the female gaze is not unique to *Outlander*, however, but can be considered part of a disturbing wider trend. Claire Cohen, writing about fan fiction, specifically slash (writing which imagines characters from favorite TV shows as gay, even if they are straight in the source text), explores the prevalence of male rape in this genre, and her findings are worth considering here. She regards fan fiction to be revealing because it provides "a way in to the active audience's thought," and hence the popularity of "non-con" (nonconsensual) slash reveals the popularity of the rape plot among women. Fans responded to and contributed to the quite explicit slash Cohen cites in a way which makes it something of a "communal project" and reveals that this is far from a deviant, minority subculture, instead reflecting the likely desires of many women, some very young. This is for her concerning because these fans, through their interest in male rape as porn—and their utilizing of a number of rape myths in the process—are "conceptualizing victimhood—for others and also for themselves" (Cohen, 2014: 106). *Outlander* may do good work around its representation of Jamie's rape, but it too is guilty of reinforcing some of these myths, perhaps with a need to appeal to its target audience, which is also largely made up of young women.

Of particular note in *Outlander* is the show's need to explain and justify Jamie not resisting Randall, a trope which is also common in non-con sex in fan fiction, as Cohen describes,

> There is a constant need to explain why the male cannot or will not fight back. . . . The former seeks to exonerate him, the latter seeks to responsiblise

him [sic], thus creating an ideal victim binary that I would argue acts to recuperate masculinity and resurrect rape myths. Thus, in this fiction for the innocent victim there is the use of extreme violence . . . and other forms of coercion, including threats of harm to family members and finally brainwashing, mind control and nervous breakdown. (2014: 106)

This explanation of how a hero comes to be so dominated by another could have been written about Jamie, who allows Randall to rape him as part of a deal to protect and free Claire—as he tells Brianna later, "I gave my word not to fight, for your mother's life"—and who soon enters a semiconscious state where he does not know where he is, due to the torture he has endured. This may seem like a positive message, acknowledging that fighting back is not a badge of honor, but it also suggests that, under "normal" circumstances, Jamie would not be raped, because he could overcome Randall had he not already agreed not to do so. This by implication then denies the real-life fact that any man can raped, no matter how "manly" or strong they might appear. Furthermore, by not allowing Jamie to resist for moral reasons, the show fails to acknowledge that sometimes fighting back is often not an option for victims. Jamie later comforts his daughter Brianna and nephew Ian after their rapes, by reassuring them that they could not have overpowered their attackers, and that their survival is itself a victory—"You did what you must to survive," as he tells Ian—but the plot does not allow Jamie himself the same reasoning. As the male lead, a rationale must be offered for his dominance by another, thus preserving his masculinity and heteronormativity. These must be restored later, too, when he finally gets revenge on Randall, though in order to be allowed to do so, the plot requires yet another male rape, as discussed below.

FERGUS AND CHILD RAPE IN *OUTLANDER*

Outlander is, then, groundbreaking in its portrayal of male rape and also makes good use of the potential television has to explore the aftermath of rape for its victims: Jamie and Ian are still dealing with, and emotionally traumatized by, their respective rapes for a full series after they occur. Unlike many shows (Anna's rape in *Downton Abbey* is a typical example), there is no sense that rape is a passing event which can be quickly recovered from, at least not for the main, male character.

Not surprisingly, part of Jamie's recovery in season 2 involves seeking revenge, if not for his own rape, then for that of his ten-year-old French ward, Fergus (Romann Berrux), who was also raped by Randall. Even Claire, once she learns from Fergus what prompted the duel between Randall and

Jamie and hence lands Jamie in a French prison, forgives her husband for breaking his previous promise to her to leave Randall alone (so that the birth of his descendant, her twentieth-century husband, Frank Randall, won't be prevented). She overhears Fergus crying and screaming "Stop!" in his sleep, and as she soothes him, he tells her, in flashback, of his waiting for Jamie in one of the brothel bedrooms; tempted by a perfume bottle which he steals, intending to later give to Claire, he is caught in the act when Randall enters the room. Surprised to see a boy rather than an adult prostitute, Randall laughingly exclaims, "You're not what I ordered . . . but you'll do," before he lunges forward to prevent Fergus's escape. Returning to the present, Fergus cries into his pillow as he tells a horrified Claire, "He wanted me to . . . I can't say it in front of a lady," and then again in flashback we see Randall turn him over, holding Fergus by his hair, as the boy cries "Stop!." When she asks why he didn't tell her sooner, he says, "I was ashamed," and she soothes him—"It's all right Fergus"—but he turns away, crying, "No, no it's not. It's all my fault." By that he means not that Randall raped him, but he believes it is his fault that Jamie is in jail: his cries for help triggered Jamie's violent reaction which ultimately led to the duel with Randall and Jamie's arrest.

In an interview after the episode aired, *Outlander*'s producer and writer, Toni Graphia, justified the graphic nature of the scene in which Randall rapes Fergus, a mere boy (which is not detailed in the book version):

> Claire was so angry and couldn't fathom why he [Jamie] broke his word, so we couldn't just hear the story too. We had to see it so we would understand. I'm proud our show doesn't shy away from showing things that are hard or ugly or brutal, but not in a way that's inorganic to the story. This scene is crucial to the story, so I stand by what we showed. We were also careful to be sensitive as well, but we wanted to do it justice. (quoted in Bucksbaum 2016)

Reactions on social media after Fergus's rape were mixed: many found it too graphic, given that Fergus is just aged ten in the series, and showing any part of it (such as Randall holding him by his hair, and thrusting into his backside) felt gratuitous to some viewers.

As we see so often in *Outlander*, the rapes of other characters ultimately are tied to Jamie and serve as an excuse for him to seek revenge against Randall for his own rape in the first season. Fergus's rape not only demands vengeance on Jamie's part but also a sacrifice from Claire. Pleading with the French king, Louis XV (Lionel Lingelser), for Jamie's release from prison, Claire "allows" the king to rape her but in telling Jamie about what occurred on the King's bed, she refers to the rape as "sleeping with" the king "to buy your freedom." Jamie replies, "Just as I gave myself to Randall to save you," thus reframing both of their rapes as mutual sacrifices. Perhaps in such a way they assume agency rather than being victims, or as Jamie explains, "It's the only way to . . . get on" (2:7). What is odd in this scene is that the rape of Fergus is not discussed, perhaps because it is too horrific for even the adults to acknowledge in words.

Of course, there is also a political element to these rapes committed by Randall, an English officer in charge of suppressing Scottish Jacobites. Depicted as a sadist (albeit a complex one) who boasts of the scars he has inflicted on Jamie with his whip in earlier scenes, he clearly represents the larger oppression of the Scottish by the British in the eighteenth century. In 2014, the prime minister at the time, David Cameron, was reported to have tried to delay the televising of *Outlander*'s first season, in an attempt to not sway the Scottish Referendum in favor of leaving the UK! (Palmer 2015). Randall's rape of a French child, too, as well as Louis XV's rape of Claire, an English woman, also have overtones of national rivalries acted out as bodily conquests. Rape in this show is frequently a metaphor for these kinds of tensions about nationhood and imperialism. Yet, while so much attention is devoted to the healing of Jamie's physical and emotional scars from his rape, Fergus's is never mentioned again, in what seems like a missed opportunity to address such a potentially traumatizing act committed against a child. Instead, the rape of Fergus is treated by *Outlander*'s writers as yet another slight against Jamie's manhood by his nemesis Randall.

CONCLUSION

All of the above rapes sparked intense debate on social media and by TV critics, perhaps because male rape is still so rare in period drama TV and thus makes for uncomfortable viewing, in a way that female rape does not. Cohen (2014) warns us that "comparing and contrasting male and female rape only fuels the continued polarization of debate and limits the conceptualization of harm, rendering male rape invisible or at least on the margins." The male rapes in *Outlander* therefore perform essential work in resisting the narrative from either rape as "just desserts" in a prison drama or as a comedy device. Abdullah-Khan (2008) observes that the stigma against male rape victims persists in the twenty-first century with a considerable lack of service provision available to men, leaving male rape victims reluctant to report offenses. #MeToo prompted not just women but male and transgender victims of sexual violence to speak out, so TV dramas like *Outlander* have the power to be part of this change. As Kilbourne concludes,

> It's useful to have a show like this illustrate these issues—even if they don't get it entirely right. . . . We need to see that men can be raped. That it's important

to talk about rape. That assault, of all kinds, can have lasting effects. It helps break down the mythology of it all. (quoted in Naugle 2019)

However, the dismissal, downplaying, and eroticization of the rape of a man by a woman in last year's most watched new drama, *Bridgerton*, remind us that this "mythology" still has a powerful hold over the popular imagination. Just like the rape of women in *Poldark* and *Banished*, this kind of assault can never be allowed to get in the way of a romance plotline—with disturbing implications for men *and* women.

NOTES

1. The case of actor Terry Crews further illustrates this point. During #MeToo he revealed he had been sexually assaulted and didn't speak out because of his hyper-masculinity and the perception that he should have done something in the moment. As a very muscular and thus "masculine" black man, he felt that he wouldn't be taken seriously as a victim. See interview in Mumford (2017), https://www.theguardian.com/film/2017/oct/11/actor-terry-crews-sexually-assaulted-by-hollywood-executive.

2. See, for example, Lisa M. Cuklanz, *Rape on Trial: How the Mass Media Construct Legal Reform and Social Change*, University of Pennsylvania Press, 1996, and Anna Wilson, *Persuasive Fictions: Feminist Narrative and Critical Myth*, Bucknell University Press, 2001.

Chapter 4

Rape as a Weapon of War
Das Boot *and* A Place to Call Home

There are perhaps more period dramas about war than any other topic, and they are traditionally very popular with audiences. The two world wars, in particular, have been the setting for a number of shows, like *The Crimson Field* (2014), *Parade's End* (2012), *World on Fire* (2019–), and series 2 of *Downton Abbey* (2010–2015), to name only a few among many more. As we have argued elsewhere, however, they usually tend to focus on the damaged bodies or minds of the men who fought in the conflict—not on women (Byrne 2015; Taddeo 2018). In this, they are simply reflecting the commonly believed, well-known cultural and historical narratives about our past. As Carol Cohn reminds us,

> There is an old story about war. It starts with war being conceived of as a quintessentially masculine realm: in it, it is men who make the decisions to go to war, men who do the planning, men who do the fighting and dying, men who protect their nation and their helpless women and children, and men who negotiate the peace, divide the spoils, and share power when war is over. In this story, women are sometimes present, but remain peripheral to the war itself. . . . The gendered reality of war is far more complex than this old story portrays. (Cohn, 2013: 1)

Like conventional war history, most war dramas tell the "story" of war from a male perspective and tend to sideline the war experiences of women. Consequently, then, they do not acknowledge conflict-related sexual violence as an important part of the suffering and trauma inflicted on women throughout human history. Recent (and hugely popular) world war films like *Dunkirk* (Nolan, 2017) and *1917* (Mendes 2019) are entirely male-focused. Unlike cinema, however, recent television has been more progressive: the shows we will examine in this chapter, *Das Boot* (2018–) and *A Place to Call*

Home (*APTCH*; 2013–2018), use rape plots as a means to shift emphasis and narrative focus to the sometimes overlooked suffering of women in wartime, in this case World War II. A reworking of the classic German film and miniseries (1981 and 1985), *Das Boot* displays a feminist undertaking to represent female war trauma parallel to that experienced by the male characters on the titular submarine. It also reflects a real shift in the unerotic representation of rape in keeping with its post-#MeToo production date. *APTCH*'s war rape narrative, while filmed on the eve of #MeToo, also calls attention to sexual violence against women as an instrument of fascism. At the same time, these shows use rape as a metaphor for the contested states that are being fought over and use the violated female body as a signifier of conflicted land and nation. Rape seems to rarely be simply about the victim in these shows: it is always a symbol of something larger and more significant, as though sexual violence against women is not enough in and of itself.

RAPE AS A WAR CRIME

The inclusion of rape plotlines in a war drama, and the resulting implication that such crimes are commonplace in war, is still radical in itself—even today. Brownmiller reminded her readers in the 1970s that rape has always accompanied conflict, but accounts of these crimes are notably absent from the history books (1975: 38). Christina Lamb's recent book *Our Bodies, Their Battlefield: What War Does to Women*, published only last year, still needs to make the argument that rape in war "is nothing new. . . . Rape is as much a weapon of war as the machete, club or Kalashnikov" but the crime has been silenced and ignored throughout human history (6). Lamb suggests that it was not until the 1990s, with the war in Bosnia, that sexual violence in conflict really reached the headlines around the world, and that the crime's visibility increased with the mass rape of women as part of the genocide in Rwanda. This led, finally, to the first international prosecution for rape as a war crime, with Jean-Paul Akayesu's conviction at the International Criminal Court:

> The first prosecution for rape as a war crime was only in 1998. . . . War rape was met with tacit acceptance and committed with impunity, military and political leaders shrugging it off as though it were a sideshow. . . . For decades it has been the world's most neglected war crime. (Lamb 2020: 8-9)

This "neglect" is particularly apparent regarding World War II, probably the most far-reaching and appalling of all twentieth-century conflicts, but one in which no prosecutions for rape were brought among the war crime tribunals in Nuremburg post-1945. It is now generally acknowledged that the Red

Army perpetuated one of the biggest mass rapes in human history when they invaded Germany at the end of the war, as explored by Antony Beevor's influential book on the subject (2004), but these (estimated as up to two million) and the thousands of other rapes committed by Allied soldiers have never been represented in popular culture or even, arguably, entered public consciousness in the same way as the atrocities of the Holocaust, for example. It is perhaps inevitable that Beevor's book was recently banned in Russia: this history of sexual violence on a huge scale is not one that any country would be likely to wish to acknowledge (Beevor, 2015). Perhaps the old adage that history is written by the victors has much to do with this, given that most, though not all, of these crimes were committed by victorious troops acting without fear of reprisal:

> It is very clear that while the Second World War might have ended for European men on 8 May 1945, the war against German women continued long after through the period of Allied Occupation . . . although much has been made of Germany's unmastered past in terms of Nazi atrocities and the Holocaust, little ink has been spilt over Allied men's unmastered past in terms of the sexual violence they unleashed on German women during the Occupation. (Teo, 1996: 192)

Even when the perpetrators are not Allies and are already identified as "villains," however, there is still a reluctance even today to discuss rape in war, as the controversy surrounding a 2011 book about the Holocaust shows. *Sexual Violence against Jewish Women during the Holocaust* (Saidel and Hedgepeth, 2011) was greeted with skepticism from influential Holocaust historians who regard rape as an insignificant part of the abuse of Jews by Nazis. Lawrence L. Langer, for example, notes that sexual violence was conspicuously absent from testimonies of survivors he had interviewed and that discussion of it risks being a distraction from the more well-documented atrocities perpetuated against the Jewish people. Langer did not ask his interviewees about rape, however, and his assumption that it would be shared freely because other horrors were may have been an erroneous one (Ravitz, 2011). Of course, the shame associated with this crime meant that it was repressed by survivors in a way other degradations were not (Sinnreich, 2010, 117). In fact, there is enough testimony from survivors who began to speak about their ordeals decades later, and other data, to confirm that sexual abuse was a reality for many Jewish prisoners (Sinnreich 2010). But the reluctance of many academics to believe rape could have been a significant part of the abuses of the Holocaust—even though every other imaginable torture had—is revealing. Some historians, like Lenore Weitzman, author of *Women in the Holocaust* (1998), were anxious about even opening up such dialogues in case "this focus on rape inappropriately sexualizes and stigmatizes female survivors" (Ravitz 2011). The shame of rape is such that it may overshadow a need to seek the truth about the past: there are, it seems, war crimes and war crimes, and rape has not traditionally formed part of the narrative we collectively wish to remember. This is beginning to change now, however, for, as Stacy Banwell notes, over the last ten years more research has been done about the experiences of Jewish women, and a new awareness of the past is being shaped (Banwell 2015, 2). And, as always, television plays an important role in disseminating these stories to a wider audience, as we will see with the recent dramas explored below.

RAPE, WAR, AND FILM

This reluctance to talk about rape as a weapon of war in "real-life" academic contexts until the twenty-first century is reflected by the representation of the crime on the big screen. Of the countless numbers of war films that were made in the twentieth century, hardly any deal with rape, no matter how graphic their depiction of the damage and violence inflicted on the (usually male) body. If rape occurs at all, it is generally only as a passing allusion. Perhaps the most famous American Holocaust film, the multiple Oscar-winning *Schindler's List* (1993), is a typical example: probably the most famous retelling of the horrors perpetuated by Nazism, this film unflinchingly represents sadistic violence and torture (inflicted on both genders) but seems to shy away from the representation of any sexual violence. Ralph Fiennes's monstrous Nazi Amon Göth is fixated by his beautiful Jewish housemaid, but although he beats and abuses her, he stops short of raping her, in line with the prevalent view of the Holocaust discussed earlier. Another successful, mainstream World War II film, *Atonement* (2007), has a rape plot as the catalyst for events, but this is a prewar rape, notably muddied by false allegations (with devastating results for the male hero) and with no interiority at all for the female victim.

Lamb's suggestion that rape in war became more visible on the political stage after the late 1990s does not, then, seem to be swiftly followed by its representation on the big screen. Since the turn of the twenty-first century, film and television began to acknowledge rape in its depiction of war only within certain, notably often non-Western, contexts. *Hotel Rwanda* (2004), for example, acknowledges rape as part of the genocide in Rwanda, as does *Sometimes in April* (2005). Period dramas about World War II, perhaps the most popular war subject matter, tend not to. The only exceptions we have found, *The Good German* (Soderbergh, 2007) and *A Woman in Berlin* (Färberböck, 2008), were not popular successes. Both deal with rape in World War II: the latter based on a memoir first published in the 1950s and controversial in Germany, which describes the rapes that followed Germany's fall to the Allied forces in 1945. Recent British rape-revenge film *The Good Liar* (2019) does include an acknowledgment that rape was a part of the postwar experience: Helen Mirren's character refers ominously to the moment in her youth "when the Russians came" and the audience understands she is referring to sexual violence. The film does not engage further with war rape, however: for the catalyst in question is again, as with *Atonement*, a prewar "date rape." As we have seen throughout this book, the film industry tends to shy away from rape in its historical dramas, and it is left to the small screen to deal with this extremely problematic issue.

DAS BOOT

Remaking classic World War II submarine film *Das Boot* (1981) was always likely to be controversial. The original West German movie (later shown as a miniseries) adapted from the 1973 novel by Lothar-Günther Buchheim and renowned for its gritty depiction of the Battle of the Atlantic as experienced in a German U-boat, had a cult following particularly among a middle-aged male audience. (An episode of the popular British sitcom *Peep Show* is based around the film, for example, as central character Mark tries to make his bored would-be girlfriend Sophie sit through all five hours of it and is baffled by her when she finally asks, "Oh, are they on a submarine?" The joke is that no woman would share, or be romanced by, his obsessive interest in the film [episode 2:5]). *Das Boot* also featured an entirely male cast and focused on their homosocial community, exploring their struggles with each other alongside their battle with the Allied forces. The recent remake, however, takes a wider perspective, interweaving the submarine focus with a parallel plot concerning the sister of one of the crewmen who is working in La Rochelle ("*Das Boot* now with added women," as a review in *The Guardian* declared [Donaghy, 2019]). This shift was considered an unnecessarily politically correct addition by some conservative fans who remained loyal to the original and disliked any deviation from it. One such example argues that "the scenes at home are literally a cheap 'hey ladies we're thinking of you moment' clearly shoehorned in at the development stage" (quoted in Donaghy, 2019). In fact, the show provides an excellent example of how adaptation can alter a source text to reflect changing gender politics and follow a more modern ideology. By following the struggles of Simone Strasser (Vicky Krieps), a Nazi translator whose loyalties are challenged after she becomes inadvertently embroiled with the French Resistance, *Das Boot* allows an exploration of female war trauma alongside the more familiar narrative of conflict among men at sea. Inevitably, in series 1, that trauma is mediated through rape. Firstly, there is the violent gang rape of a minor character, which is overlooked and downplayed by most of the characters but actually has far-reaching repercussions for the plot, then the rape of a Jewish captive, and in the final episode there is the violent attempted rape of Simone herself.

Three rape plotlines in an eight-part series, plus some examples of coercive sex which as we will discuss later can be identified as on the "rape spectrum," make sexual violence a key part of the show. In fact, casual misogyny and jokes about sexual misconduct are apparent in this right from the beginning and the German navy is throughout constructed, probably with historical accuracy, as a macho male culture with little respect for women and hence the potential for violence. Thus, the rapes, when they occur, are not individualized and not especially about individual characters. Rather, they feel like part and parcel of a culture that devalues and mistreats women verbally and physically. Notably, none of the rapes feel gratuitous: there is no nudity, and it is violence rather than sex which is emphasized throughout.

The first victim is Nathalie (Clara Ponsot), who is secretly Jewish and secretly married to Simone's brother, but works as a barmaid in La Rochelle, and is raped at work by a group of belligerent German soldiers returning from a mission. Prostitutes are in plentiful supply in this bar, as they seem to be everywhere in the port, but the ready availability of other sexual partners is not sufficient for the soldier who accosts her instead. The message is clear here that this rape and indeed all the rapes in the show are not about sex, but about the expectation that all female bodies should be available for male use, at all times. There is no line between sex workers and other women in the eyes of almost all the soldiers in the show. Moreover, this rape is an act of revenge: it takes place because Nathalie is French, and the Resistance have just bombed a celebration party for their returning U-boat. Hence her body becomes a symbol of the enemy and has to be punished as such:

> "She says she only works down here and doesn't fuck. Girl, that feels as wrong as a bomb going off in a safe harbour. If you won't go upstairs with me we do it right here. . . . Fucking French whore. You do what you are told." (episode 1:3)

In these wars over land and nationality, the victim's body is territory to be conquered: there is a clear overlap with the rape plots in *Outlander* here. Indeed, Nathalie's attack encapsulates all the ways rape can be used as a weapon of war. It is strategic, for, as Carol Cohn argues, "A core aspect of hegemonic masculinity in most societies is men's control over and protection of their wives and daughters, the rape of male opponents' women can be seen as an effective way of unmanning/disempowering these men" (Cohn 11). It is also, as well as revenge and punishment, a reward.

The crew have just returned from a dangerous, successful mission, and as Brownmiller reminds us, "Down through the ages, triumph over women by rape became a way to measure victory, part of a soldier's proof of masculinity and success, a tangible reward for services rendered" (1975: 35). Nathalie's attack is hence loaded with political meaning, but her identity as a person and a victim is lost in it all: she never recovers consciousness, and so never speaks about her suffering. She has tried to stay on the periphery of this war, hiding in plain sight and almost literally keeping her head down throughout the Occupation, but this strategy for survival ultimately fails. Hence it is significant that her rape becomes the catalyst for Simone's increasing involvement in the conflict, as the latter realizes it is impossible to remain detached. After coming to an understanding of the crime, Simone changes allegiance, joins the Resistance—significantly it is a female-led cell—and begins to assist them against the occupying forces. These are, however, actions which will eventually lead to her own rape plotline. For all women in this series, to be female in wartime is to come up against rape sooner or later.

We have mentioned a link with *Outlander*, and another thing that these two very different shows have in common is the public nature of Nathalie's rape, which takes place on a table in full view of the rest of the bar. This is even more public than Brianna's attack, but, like hers, no one in the bar intervenes. The presence of bystanders signifies the way society is complicit in this crime, which, as we discussed in chapter 2, is becoming particularly important in the post-#MeToo representation of rape. It is notable here that Nathalie's female as well as male coworkers in the bar not only fail to come to her assistance but later blame her for provoking the attack. Simone visits the scene of the crime next morning, seeking answers, and is shocked at the response of the female pub owner:

"What happened?"
"Bobby Shluz's men . . . they wanted to have fun."
"And the barmaid, Nathalie? What happened to her?"
"She always thought she was so much better than anybody else. If she had played along nothing much would have happened. But she had to fight and yell. She got a dressing down. And we have to close up for a week." (episode 1:4)

Of course, Nathalie receives rather more than a "dressing down": she later dies from her injuries. But the underplaying of, and refusal to name, the crime is not confined to this one deeply unsympathetic character. So shameful is rape that the word cannot be spoken out loud, even by Margot, the French nurse who cares for Nathalie: "She is seriously injured. Head—and lower abdomen. They were German. But we were ordered not to talk about it" (episode 1:4). Even she and her fellow hospital staff, in their discretion and fear, contribute to the silencing that surrounds the crime. As a result, of course, no punishment is sought and no justice brought. Later, when it is revealed—unsurprisingly, given the way rape is viewed as a "reward for services rendered"—that complicity reverberates high up into the German navy, a superior officer dismisses Nathalie as "just a French whore," echoing the same phrase used by the perpetrators themselves, and instead of disciplining his men he only jokes, "Hopefully you didn't catch the clap." The hypermasculine, "boys will be boys" culture here not only silences rape but condones and encourages it. Only Simone herself seeks retribution, but the assistance she brings to the Resistance makes minimal impact on the Occupying forces and serves only to bring her own body under threat from sexual violence.

Simone's rape plotline is less straightforward, and for viewers less familiar, than Nathalie's. She is pursued romantically by her boss, Gestapo officer, Hagen Forster (Tom Wlaschiha), who is the antihero of the show. It is initially unclear whether she finds him attractive, but as the series progresses it becomes apparent she is humoring his attentions because of his powerful position and her anxiety about her own, increasingly compromised one. Eventually she has sex with him which appears consensual but is actually deeply problematic when viewed from a #MeToo perspective, given the power imbalance of their relationship. Hsu-Ming Teo's discussion of the range of sexual abuse experienced by German women at the end of the war is useful to recall here:

> The concept of a continuum of sexual violence is useful for a study of German women's experiences in Zero Hour for the following reasons. Firstly, it can be used to conceptualise German women's sexual experiences, ranging from consensual sex (equally desired by woman and man), to altruistic sex (women do it because they feel sorry for the man or guilty about saying no), to compliant sex (the consequences of not doing it are worse than the consequences of doing it), to rape. (1996: 193)

Simone's experience with Forster clearly fits under this definition of "compliant sex": she sleeps with him primarily because she is frightened and hopes by doing so to avoid his suspicion. This plotline hence reminds the viewer that rape is indeed a "continuum": any ambiguity about their relationship is finally removed in the last episode of series 1 when Simone reveals that she did not enjoy it and is in fact in love with another woman. The viewer might have some sympathy for Forster at this point, given he wishes to marry Simone and had no idea he was being used, but any identification with the character is short-lived as he then attempts to violently rape her in revenge (See figure 4.1). This act—only halted when she stabs him—implies that all the seemingly romantic interactions that have gone before are just part of the

Figure 4.1 Simone's Coercive Relationship with Forster Ends in Rape, in *Das Boot*, Episode 1:8 (2018). *Source*: Screen grab by Katherine Byrne.

same narrative of ownership and control. Moreover, Forster horribly punishes her for her lack of compliance later, in series 2, when he withholds medical care and morphine when she is dying of a gunshot wound. It is notable that rape is equated to death for women again and again in this series. Nathalie dies from the injuries inflicted by the rape, and Simone, while able to walk away physically from her ordeal, loses her mental equilibrium and survival instinct following it. By series 2, she appears to be accepting of, or is even pursuing, death, and finally willingly sacrifices herself for the Jewish family she is helping to escape. In contrast, Forster, and the other rapists in the show, survive and thrive. Bleak though this might seem, it is in fact an accurate reflection of the horrible consequences of rape in war. Some 10,000 German women died following their rape during the fall of Berlin: some from their injuries, like Nathalie, and some because they committed suicide, which is effectively what Simone does. In this way, the show seems to acknowledge the terribly high price women paid for Allied victory.

MEN WHO RAPE

One of the show's most disturbing, but most important, messages is that it is not just certain types of men who rape, but all men, given the circumstances. We know nothing of the submariners who rape Nathalie before their crime, but immediately prior to it witness their excessive drinking, public indecency, and casual misogyny, and assume villainous tendencies and contempt for the law. Hagen Forster is rather different, however. Despite being a member of the Nazi party, he is a relatively moral and moderate figure in series 1, counseling mercy and restraint about treatment of the French. Notably he also, unlike many of his colleagues, condemns the actions of Nathalie's rapists, until he himself joins their ranks. Even more disturbing, however, is when a previously gentle character proves themselves capable of rape. Like the women in the show, Thorsten Hecker (Leon Lukas Blaschke) is a victim of the macho culture in the German military. The youngest and most innocent of the crew of U-612, he is anxious and ashamed when his bullying friends bring him to a prostitute the night before they leave port, and as a result he does not consummate the encounter they set up for him. Given the superstition on the boat that holds that a virgin is bad luck, however, he comes to believe that he is responsible for all the problems he and the crew have experienced from this point on, and when the crew come across a mysterious stranded ship with some Jewish prisoners inside, he sees an opportunity to rectify this. This is one of the only moments in series 1 which deals in any way with the implications of the Holocaust (series 2 addresses this in much more detail) and it is notable that rape is key to the narrative. One of the prisoners is a teenage girl, and has been kept, tied up, separate from her family, we assume specifically for "usage" by the crew. This plot seems a political statement which goes against the narrative of *Rassenschande* which suggests that Jewish women were "safe" from rape by Germans because they were beneath contempt for Aryans (Friedman 2002). This terrified girl has presumably been raped many times by the crew, and Thorsten too does not even contemplate her Jewishness: she is simply there to be taken. Initially sympathetic, he starts to free her, but then thinks better of it and, promising not to hurt her, and explaining to her that he has to because "it is all his fault" that people have died on the boat, rapes her instead. A confrontation between the crews immediately follows this, and the girl is shot dead, taking a bullet that was meant for Thorsten: just more, female collateral damage in this war.

This whole episode makes very distressing viewing, partly because the ship's cargo hold proves to be filled with Jewish refugees who have paid for safe passage to Canada and who, in an uncomfortable reminder of the plight of so many real, current-day migrants, have almost all died in transit. The only ones still living are the girl's parents who kill themselves when they learn their daughter has not survived. They, at least, care about her fate: no one else mentions her again, and it is another example of rape in the show which goes unpunished. There is no condemnation of these events, and no further discussion of them, but Thorsten's friend is killed in the shoot-out, and his dying words—that it was perhaps *he* that was bad luck—can be read as an acknowledgment that his aggressively macho attitude has not done his friends or himself any favors, and has contributed to a toxic culture with terrible consequences for women.

Das Boot, therefore, inserts back into history a reality often omitted from it: that rape has always accompanied war, and that one of the most oft-revisited wars, World War II, is no exception. This is the flip side to the champagne drinking glamour and devil-may-care courage that are most often the picture of this war on screen. This was a conflict which, for those on the winning side at least, is a story of triumph over the evils of fascism, and which has not been allowed to be tainted by the evil which was perpetuated on both sides, against women. It might be not accidental then that the show which most frequently represents rape is made by a German company and is hence less invested in this narrative of heroism. Indeed, *Das Boot* as a whole is distrustful of the pursuit of honor, which it often represents as reckless or self-interested. It is the quietest, most cerebral characters, the least aggressively macho, and often the least obviously patriotic who are the most sympathetic in this show: Simone's brother Frank and his captain Hoffman. But they are in the minority and in most cases unsuitable for the navy: it is not accidental that survival for both of them involves leaving the boat, and the German Navy, behind in series 2.

The show's representation of rape, then, implies agreement with an argument expressed by Brownmiller, in which she suggests war is not a cause but an opportunity:

> Rape in war is a familiar act with a familiar excuse. War provides men with the perfect backdrop to give vent to their contempt for women. The very maleness of the military—the brute power of weaponry exclusive to their hands, the spiritual bonding of men at arms, the manly discipline of orders given and orders obeyed, the simple logic of the hierarchical command—confirms for men what they long suspect, that women are peripheral, irrelevant to the world that counts. . . . Men who rape in war are ordinary Joes, made unordinary by entry into the most exclusive male-only club in the world. (1975: 32)

Brownmiller's feminist anger here does not believe that war brutalizes men and removes the moral compass that prevents rape; rather, she holds that all men are potential rapists and that conflict simply facilitates and encourages this. *Das Boot* does implicitly support this message: in the homosocial macho culture of the German navy, women have become only objects. Furthermore, by making seemingly "good" respectable characters rape alongside more conventionally villainous ones, the message seems to be that any, or at least many, men can become such, given the opportunity. It is true, of course, that little or no judgment is meted out to any of those who rape, by their friends, colleagues, or superiors, and this lack of morality is problematic, especially given that their victims end up paying the ultimate price. While the world of the show tolerates rape, however, the audience is invited to have a very different perspective. If, as Brownmiller states, one of the key reasons for rape in war is the male belief in their superiority and centrality, this show sets out to show that women are not peripheral or "irrelevant" at all. As much time in the series is given to Simone on land as to her brother and the crew of U-811 at sea, and while their adventures are mostly centered on their own survival, hers is a more heroic narrative of self-sacrifice. When she and her brother are tearfully reunited in the final moments of the series, both have undergone significant hardships and traumas, but only hers are entirely in the service of others. She has repeatedly and, we learn in series 2, permanently sacrificed her security and well-being for him, for Nathalie, for their baby daughter, and for the people of La Rochelle. The show then utilizes certain conventions about rape but is deeply unconventional in its assertion that war is, in fact, about women, too—and that they can, in fact, be more than just victims.

RAPE AS WAR CRIME IN *APTCH*

So far in this chapter the focus has been on a non-British period drama. The reason is quite simple: as noted earlier, the dominant narrative in British period series about victims of war consistently revolves around male soldiers' struggles with shell shock/PTSD. British soldiers as the perpetrators of sexual violence against women—either as civilians on the home front or as members of auxiliary military organizations—are noticeably absent despite the rampant and very real sexual aggressions committed by Allied men against British and American women in wartime (Gubar 1987). Allied propaganda portrayed "the enemy"—both German and Japanese—as first and foremost a rapist: carrying off the partially clad Aryan looking woman as the bounty of war. Yet, as Gubar has shown, much of the sexual violence directed against Allied women who served in organizations like the WAAF was at the hands of their male compatriots, as well as other malicious acts such as sabotaging their equipment and vehicles with the intention of physically harming them. Yet while these accounts were documented by women fiction writers after the war, they remain absent from period dramas which instead showcase women's heroism on the home front or their victimization by the Fascist enemy.

Of course, we have seen uniformed British men commit rape in eighteenth-century themed dramas like *Outlander*, in which Black Jack Randall's repeated assaults on the Fraser clan is used as shorthand for English oppression of the Scottish Highlanders, and in *Banished*, in which female convicts are used as sexual slaves by British soldiers and officers alike in the New South Wales penal colony. While rape is definitely a weapon of war in these dramas, it is not presented as such in more recent conflicts—like World War II—in which British national identity is, and has ever since been, bound up with a narrative of heroism. Even in *Home Fires* (2015–2016), a drama about women volunteers on the village home front in World War II, the only act of sexual violence involves a case of marital rape, rather than a war crime.

In *Bletchley Circle*'s (2012–2014) first season, female codebreakers reunite in 1952 London to catch a serial rapist and killer, whose crimes are caused by war-induced trauma, and so a story about violence against women ultimately points back to war's deleterious impact on the men who served. While another recent British war drama, *World on Fire* (2019–), offers a more nuanced view of the atrocities committed by both sides in the war, the acts of sexual violence against women in the series are committed solely by Nazis.

Yet another example in which rape as a weapon of war is used not by the Allies but by Nazis alone is in the popular Australian series, *APTCH*. *APTCH* has a large viewing audience in the United Kingdom and the United States, and unlike *Das Boot*, its soap opera format targets a predominantly female audience. Set in rural New South Wales (also the setting of *Banished*, discussed in chapter 1), the series follows Sarah Adams (Marta Dusseldorp) who has returned to her home country after twenty years abroad and her ensuing involvement with the local wealthy Bligh family. Set in the 1950s, the shadow of World War II looms large over its key female protagonist, the details of which are revealed gradually throughout the first two seasons. Through flashbacks we learn that as a young woman, Sarah had left Australia for Paris where she married a French Jew for whom she converted; together she and Rene worked for the Resistance during the war until they were arrested and interred in separate camps. As a beautiful blonde she escaped the fate of other Jewish camp inmates when she was chosen by the Nazi guards to "service" them instead. It is notable that we learn very little about Sarah's work in the Resistance movement: instead of details of her heroism from the war, we encounter her primarily as a rape victim. This does rather undermine the narrative of proto-feminism that runs through the show—Sarah achieves independence through her nursing work after the war, but does not seem to be allowed any during it—but at least she survives, unlike all the victims of war rape we see in *Das Boot*. "Those who resisted were shot," she tells her aunt, but by following orders she avoids their fate.

Recalling her past to George Bligh (Brett Climo), to whom she is now engaged, she prefaces her account by noting, "You have to understand the depth of my love for Rene to understand what I did" (episode 2:5). This particular scene was billed in the episode preview as "The confession he never saw coming"; indeed Sarah fears "it will be the end of us"—that George can "never forgive her." The word "rape" is never used, but these were certainly repeated rapes—Sarah was a prisoner of war—and George reassures her that "there's no shame when there's no choice." Nevertheless, he is tormented by Sarah's "confession," and here the rape fantasy becomes his own as he admits to Sarah in a later scene that "I can't get these images out of my mind. . . . All those men." When we see the rapes through George's eyes, Sarah is now lying on a sheeted bed, in silk stockings, looking pleased as a toned German arm strokes her body, and she moans. Sarah angrily reminds George, "There was no pleasure, it was only violence and horror," so that George, admonished over his reaction, promises her that he will "come to terms with it."

In giving us George's point of view, the series complicates the male gaze—not to empower George but to make *him* feel vulnerable. He tells Sarah that he feels helpless and angry, that he wasn't there to help the woman he loves, even though he didn't even know her during the war. While it is easy for us to lump this rape narrative into the countless others on TV in which the rape is used to focus on the male reaction, what makes this one unique is that George cannot seek revenge against Sarah's aggressors. The war is long over and as a politician George has preached reconciliation with Australia's former enemies. Instead, this subplot underscores how war-induced PTSD is not solely a masculine affair but also how these types of war crimes impact Sarah's future and her new family.

Just as important, *APTCH* shows the viewer what has only in recent years been emerging as a truth about sexual violence in concentration camps. As we discussed earlier, the emphasis in Holocaust studies has been not on rape, but as Beverley Chalmers notes, "on how Jewish women had kept their families together and functioning after their husbands and fathers had lost their jobs, been arrested, sent to concentration camps, or killed" (2016). As Chalmers explains, "Survivors didn't talk about anything having to do with sex because they didn't want their children and grandchildren to know what had happened to them." While rape was never an official Nazi policy, the German camps used Jewish women in brothels designated for military, SS (like the one in which Sarah is shown), and foreign workers. Sarah's story brings home to the viewer the ongoing damage done to families and survivors, even many years after the war ends. Discovering she is pregnant with George's child in series 2, we learn through a dream sequence that this is not her first, or maybe not even her second, pregnancy, the others resulting from her time in the concentration camps. We see the back of a uniformed Nazi carrying away her crying newborn, presumably to be killed (as most Jewish offsprings were) or, if lucky, adopted by German parents. Sarah's own surprise over her latest pregnancy suggests she believed herself left sterile from the repeated rapes (or from medical experimentation, which is documented as taking place at Ravensbruck: in all camps, of course, many inmates were forcibly sterilized). She confides to her boss and friend, Dr. Jack Duncan (Craig Hall), that she's considering terminating the pregnancy, fearing that something might "be wrong" with the child because she's "impure" from the rapes: "How can anything good grow inside of me?" she asks. Ultimately Sarah decides not to end the pregnancy and after the revelation to her fiancé George about her prison camp experiences, she commits to raising her child in the Jewish faith, a testament to the failure of the Nazis to destroy her. As such, she is an unusual example: a survivor of war rape who goes on to thrive.

WAR RAPE AND NATIONAL IDENTITY

Sarah's experiences in *APTCH* show us yet again the important work performed by period drama television as it addresses the suffering of victims and highlights stories which have been overlooked by other narratives about the past—including, in this case, those in our history books. That said, however, this bringing out of new or alternative truths is flawed: in *APTCH*, as in many British dramas, some truths are more palatable than others. Sarah's experiences are constructed by the show in very specific terms, and they locate the source of war rape as being very far from home. For example, we see her, in one flashback scene, lying on a stained, sheetless narrow bed, staring dead-eyed into space, when one officer leaves and another enters the room, turns on the phonograph, and "Silent Night" plays in German as he proceeds to undress (See figure 4.2). The camera does not show us the rape but focuses instead on his hat, the distinctive cap of the German army. It is implied that this is one of the many rapes Sarah has endured as a prisoner of war, and the message is clear: this is a Nazi crime, one of several forms of sexual violence perpetuated against the Allies in the show (her friend and colleague Jack, who is also a survivor of a war camp, has also been sexually tortured by the Japanese, which leaves him physically and emotionally scarred and dependent on alcohol: we discuss how Jack's experience becomes blurred with that of his fiancée's rape in chapter 2).

Of course, this plot does important work in acknowledging the often overlooked horrors of war against women, and especially against Jewish women, as we discussed earlier. But in showing the viewer Sarah's rape (and Jack's torture) as a crime committed by the Opposition, the show does seem to "other" sexual violence, constructing it as being committed only by non-Allied men. Unlike *Das Boot*, which acknowledges that conflict and a misogynistic environment can turn any man into a rapist, *APTCH* overlooks or represses the sex crimes committed not only by Allies in general but by Australians in particular. As Joanna Bourke notes, Australian men were infamous for the rapes they carried out during and after the war in the Pacific: "In the words of a Japanese prostitute talking about soldiers who had landed at Kure, the port of Hiroshima . . . 'The Australian soldiers were the worst . . . For such actions the Australian troops earned the disreputable name 'Yabanjin' or 'Barbarians'" (2007: 357–358). Significantly, though unsurprisingly, the reporting of these rapes caused problems for Australian national identity. Of course, after the war many Japanese servicemen were court-martialed for rapes and other war

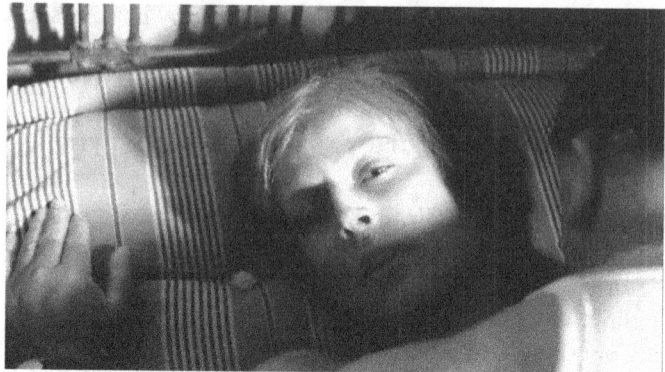

Figure 4.2   Sarah's Flashback to Her Time at Ravensbrück Camp in *A Place to Call Home*, Episode 2:5 (2014). *Source*: Screen grab by Julie Anne Taddeo.

crimes, but the dominant narrative constructed this as their failing, one of the things Allies were fighting the war against. Rape, of course, was not part of the persona that Allied forces wished to present:

> The mass rapes of these Japanese women only came to the attention of the authorities when they were considered to threaten the image of democracy that the occupation forces were attempting to encourage. . . . Back in Australia the commission of sexual atrocities was being denied as late as the 1990s. When a report on the rapes of 1945 was published in The Age in September 1993, uproar followed. . . . The "Aussie" male's protective stance towards weaker women was under attack. The rapes exposed something truly despotic in the Australian myth. (Bourke, 2007: 358)

It is hard not to consider Sarah's rape plot as a response to these ongoing anxieties about Australian manhood, given it is clearly othered, taking place elsewhere, and committed by nameless, faceless men of a different nationality. The men of *APTCH* are there to comfort and support their wives (and in Jack's case, avenge them, as we discuss in chapter 2). There is no sense that they, or their friends, might have committed similar crimes during their service, or have been part of the same epidemic of sexual violence in conflict—yet history clearly shows that they were.

CONCLUSION

Women's experience of war in period drama has traditionally been a celebration of their home front endeavors: making do on rations, tilling the land vacated by male farmers, a romance with a soldier on leave, and volunteering as nurses. But the recent dramas discussed in this chapter suggest how much more complex, varied, and traumatic war was—and is—for women. Both the shows discussed here write "back into history" the sexual violence which, sadly, was a daily reality for women in conflict zones around the world, and still is today. Whether the horrors of total war turn decent men into monsters, or, as Brownmiller suggests, gives them the freedom to satisfy their hatred of women, rape is at once a weapon and a reward for those who served in the armed forces. *Das Boot*, a show which critiques concepts of heroism and jingoism, acknowledges this. *APTCH* locates it firmly elsewhere, in a Nazi concentration camp along with more familiar war crimes, and in doing so represses the many rapes committed by the Allies themselves. But as national identity in the West has been, since 1945, so bound up with the narrative of justified victory and moral superiority that emerged out of World War II (and continues to dominate its commemoration), it is unsurprising that most dramas prefer to ignore this uncomfortable reality. Instead, Allied nations have traditionally represented themselves as protectors and liberators of the vulnerable—ignoring the fact that, for women, all wars are crimes.

Chapter 5

Procurement and Period Drama
Rape for Money in Harlots

In the other chapters of this book, we have examined the many ways in which our society has long ignored, condoned, justified, or even encouraged rape. One of the oldest and most endemic ways in which the crime has been socially sanctioned, however, occurs when there is money to be made from it. The procurement of unwilling and often underage girls for sexual abuse is one of the darkest aspects of the global sex trade that has flourished throughout human history. (We engage only briefly in this chapter in wider debates about consent and prostitution, which are largely beyond the scope of this book: by "rape for money" we primarily mean the abuse of those who are trafficked into the sex trade.) Recent events in the media show the extent to which this kind of institutionalized sexual abuse has long been big business: the Weinstein and Epstein cases, for example, have revealed the way in which procurement, money, and power have intersected. In this regard *Harlots* (2017–), a drama about prostitution in eighteenth-century London, in which rape is commonplace and lucrative to the point of being auctioned to the highest bidder, can be considered a powerful social commentary, as this chapter will explore. As we will discuss below, this critically acclaimed, female-dominated show features many sex workers who have agency over their lives but also has characters who are denied a choice and are raped as part of the sex trade. It thus examines the motivations of men and women who benefit financially from sexual crime and the institutional and pervasive nature of rape for money. Of course, TV's representation of rape as business is complicated by its own exploitation of the crime for ratings, and this show displays an awareness of this problematic culpability, a point we will return to.

Chapter 5

PROCUREMENT IN CONTEMPORARY CULTURE

The horrors of rape for sale have come to public attention and censure at certain key moments over the centuries. In the 1880s in Britain, for example, journalist W. T. Stead wrote a series of articles in *The Pall Mall Gazette*, entitled "The Maiden Tribute of Modern Babylon." Stead exposed how commonplace the "white slave trade" in virgins was when he infamously, and easily, purchased a thirteen-year-old girl who had been abducted for his use (Walkowitz 1992). Respectable Victorian London was horrified by his revelations and Stead's "government by journalism" did prompt Parliament to raise the age of consent to sixteen in 1885, but in real terms this exposé—and the laws passed in both Britain and the United States aimed at combatting sex trafficking—made little difference to the success of a trade which still thrives today. Thousands of children and women of all nationalities are exploited for sex by organized crime every year in Britain alone, but as investigative journalist Lydia Cacho notes, this is a worldwide problem:

> All over the planet, we are witnessing a culture that considers the kidnapping, disappearance, trade and corruption of young girls and adolescents as normal. . . . Each year, 1.39 million people around the world—mostly women and girls—are subjected to sexual slavery. . . . Sexual pleasure feeds economic and political power. . . . Sexual pleasure is a great tool of cohesion and negotiation among groups of males in the military and business, to such an extent that the sex trade is the most profitable in the world, even more than the arms and drugs trades. (Cacho, 2014: 3–5)

Rape for profit is, and always has been, big business, as this chapter will discuss. Moreover, as with rape in war (as discussed in chapter 4), it is a crime which has to be silenced and sanctioned by governments and authorities in order to thrive. This is perfectly illustrated by one of the most famous abuse trials of recent years: the Jeffrey Epstein case. Epstein's crimes came to light from 2005 onward, when he was first accused of abusing a fourteen-year-old girl, and in 2008 he pleaded guilty to the procurement of a child. Likely due to his money and powerful connections, however, this initial thirteen-month sentence was carried out under the lightest restrictions possible, even though he had now faced numerous accusations which were mostly settled out of court. It was not until 2019 that he was arrested again on charges of trafficking dozens of girls, some as young as twelve, and offering them to his friends for sex. He committed suicide in his prison cell in 2019, but since his death—which his lawyers have alleged involved foul play—his links with other powerful figures have been uncovered, most notably a friendship with Great Britain's Prince Andrew and with Jean-Luc Brunel, the head of the

Paris modeling agency, Karin Models, who is himself under investigation by French police (Willsher 2020). The case continues, and likely involves many more high-profile people. Particular media attention and fascination has, however, focused on the role played by Epstein's former girlfriend and long-time companion Ghislaine Maxwell, who allegedly procured many underage girls for him throughout their friendship:

> Since Epstein's death in August 2019 while in custody on charges of sex trafficking minors, and since her own arrest on 2 July, the spotlight on Maxwell, 58, has been relentless. The public's appetite for news about the youngest child of the late press baron Robert Maxwell has been insatiable. Fascination has been fuelled by the Netflix documentary Jeffrey Epstein: Filthy Rich. Then there is the "she-devil" factor. Helena Kennedy, the former junior counsel to Myra Hindley, has argued that women accused of sexual crimes can garner greater public opprobrium than men. (Davies 2020)

Maxwell's involvement is of particular interest to the public because she is unusual as a woman complicit in, rather than only a victim of, these systems of money, abuse, and power, and because she clearly profited from them. This fascination with the women who exploit or abuse, rather than aid, their own sex has become a stalwart of modern culture—see also Queen Bee syndrome (Reality Check, 2018)—and similarly there has long been a fascination with the "Madam," the female brothel owner. Hence Maxwell has become the face of the Epstein scandal, long before she was actually tried in 2021 for involvement in his crimes (see, for example, the recent Sky documentary, *Epstein's Shadow: Ghislaine Maxwell* [2021]). This interest in the women who facilitate or encourage systems of sexual abuse by men, for a variety of reasons, is one of the key themes in *Harlots*, as we will explore in this chapter.

PROSTITUTION ON SCREEN: *HARLOTS*

First aired in 2017, *Harlots*' broadcast followed the civil suits taken against Epstein and Maxwell by a number of women, most famously Virginia Giuffre in 2015. *Harlots*' focus is on sex work generally, but several of its subplots deal with procurement of unwilling girls, and thus can be considered a response to those events, as well as a reminder of the long and dark history of rape for sale. The show, which is created and directed by women, has been described as "the bawdiest drama BBC has ever aired" (Kavanagh, 2020). It is based on historian Hallie Rubenhold's account of prostitution in Georgian London, *The Covent Garden Ladies*, which draws on the infamous "Harris's List," an annual "guide" to the prostitutes of London which for nearly fifty years described their charms in lurid detail (credited to Samuel Derrick, published 1757 to 1795). Originally broadcast on *ITV Encore* in 2017, *Harlots* reached a wider audience when it was bought by the BBC and shown there in 2020, and now has a cult following, with a number of fan sites devoted to the show.

In their study of sexual violence in eighteenth-century women's novels, Dowd-Arrow and Creel have written about the similarities that exist between how women were abused then and now, and the shocking lack of progress that has been achieved in the last 300 years or so:

> For a generation "fatigued" with feminism, the eighteenth century provides a ripe teaching ground within the historical scope of feminist endeavours, if we highlight the similarities between those cultural issues young women face today which are so evident in many texts by early eighteenth-century women writers. (Dowd-Arrow and Creel 2016: 1)

For Dowd-Arrow and Creel, the rhetoric and justification and excusing of rape is relatively unchanged over history (as we discuss further in chapter 1) and then as now, women's voices and stories are the best way to understand and access it. *Harlots* follows the fortunes and quarrels of two rival brothels and their warring female owners, played with great relish by Samantha Morton and Leslie Manville, and chronicles the lives of a wide spectrum of sex workers from different social backgrounds. Its central plot is the relationship between these female leads, and their (but especially Manville's Quigley) willingness to exploit other women to thrive and survive, in a way which definitely recalls Ghislaine Maxwell. Indeed, this is one of the key objections feminist critics have made about the show:

> One of the problematic narrative issues with *Harlots* is its focus on women tearing down other women, which seems counterproductive when they're all dealing with lives that are already hard enough as it is. . . . Nevertheless, in this way, it is realistic. One of the many results of the current #MeToo movement is the revelation of just how much women, driven by trying to advance or survive in a patriarchal world, have helped to perpetuate the abuse and oppression of fellow women. (Nguyen, 2018)

In most of the other shows explored in this book it is men, and the patriarchy which empowers them, which are the problem: women may be complicit by their silence, but that is all. Here, however, women are as much to blame as the clients whose lusts they set out to satisfy—even if they are, of course, somewhat absolved by being themselves also victims. Despite this cynical view of those high up the food chain, however, the show has been acclaimed by other critics for its nuanced handling of sex work, which in the show is both a source of abuse and a means of financial independence and social mobility for all the female characters: "[*Harlots*] is a criminally overlooked post #MeToo feminist triumph, created by and starring women and for once, focusing on the brutality of prostitution without reducing it to a load of actually quite sexy sex" (Ramaswamy, 2019). Certainly, *Harlots* does not represent commercial sex as in any way erotic, nor just as a stepping-stone to a better life. In this it differs dramatically from most portrayals of sex work on screen which, as Rochelle Dalla argues,

> often portray prostitution as a temporary course of action, where in the end the heroine finds love and happiness and suffers few, if any, enduring scars from her brief stint on the streets; an image not borne out by empirical research and the realities of drug use, homelessness and the multiple challenges of leaving prostitution that women face. (2000: 352)

Dalla cites Hollywood films like *Pretty Woman* (1990) and *Leaving Las Vegas* (1995) as good examples of this kind of romanticizing of sex work. Generally, British television is not much better, given how *Secret Diary of a Call Girl* (2007–2011) glamorized and eroticized the profession. In contrast to this, the prostitutes in *Harlots* have no easy way out, and no romantic rescue from a male lead is forthcoming for them: in each case, they have to work through their own problems. Charlotte Wells's (Jessica Brown Findlay, in a very different role from *Downton Abbey*'s Lady Sybil!) handsome lover Daniel looks as though he might "rescue" her from a life of sin, but actually he is powerless, impoverished, and Irish, and it is she who must save him from prison in the final episode of the first series. We expect *Harlots* to be a Fanny-Hill-esque narrative of social mobility, but it is in fact more complex and more dark, as most characters improve their status and then lose that security again. Indeed, it could be argued that this period drama is unique for its gritty portrayal of the sex industry, without falling into any of the other clichés normally associated with a realistic representation of it (often as those forced into the profession because of drug addiction, another stereotype many researchers have disproved).

Most interesting for our purposes, however, are the ways in which the show uses the rape culture of the eighteenth century to insert itself into debates about agency and choice which still dominate discourse about the sex industry today. As Maddy Coy has discussed, writing about sex work centers around

> the question of whether prostitution itself is harmful for the bodily integrity and autonomy of women who sell sex, or harm created by the conditions in which

prostitution operates . . . for many there is not a simple dichotomy; criminalization and stigmatization of women involved in prostitution intensifies harm and stigmatization. (Coy 2012: 1)

For example, sex-positive feminists like Kelly J. Bell argue that it is not helpful to think of prostitution as intrinsically "harmful" at all, but rather it should be legal and socially accepted because

> *sex work is essentially just work* . . . it is not necessarily harmful to women. Under circumstances in which sex work is accepted and regulated in society, in which the sex worker is protected and granted the same rights as any other laborer, sex work has the possibility to be beneficial to women. . . . Every human being has the right to make informed decisions about his or her own body, and laws that govern sex work are laws that govern an individual's right to make decisions about her own body. (2009, emphasis added)

Not all feminists agree with this view: others argue that prostitution is, and always has been, a form of sexual violence and that pervasive cultural beliefs that women partake in it freely only serve to conceal the reality of a life filled with suffering. This is especially pertinent in relation to poorer societies: Farley et al., in their exploration of PTSD in contemporary sex workers, point out that

> prostitution has been increasingly normalized in many cultures where, whether legal or not, it is promoted or tolerated as a reasonable job for women. . . . Instead of the question, "Did she voluntarily consent to prostitution?" the more relevant question would be: "Did she have real alternatives to prostitution for survival?" (2003)

Of course, this viewpoint implies that other kinds of paid work undertaken purely for survival is in some way better or more acceptable than prostitution, which indeed may not be the case: life and labor under capitalism frequently problematizes the whole notion of consent. *Harlots*, significantly, asks all these kinds of questions in an eighteenth-century context, and while not providing answers, makes the audience reflect on sex work then and today. The show sets out to demythologize prostitution, but also represents it as "a reasonable job for women," in that most of the characters appear philosophical and good-humored about their work and take pride in their skills. Sex performed for money may not always be enjoyable, but it is represented as a potentially less demeaning profession than other, more menial jobs. Most transactions are depicted here as routine, conventional encounters, consensual—with the economic provisos indicated later—and while certainly not romanticized, faintly comic. One or two characters even appear to have some romantic interest in their "regulars," including the central character, Margaret Wells (Samantha Morton), who has had a relationship with a client (Nathaniel Lennox, played by Col O'Neill) who it is joked she used to give it to "for free" (episode 2). Pleasure and commercial sex are not mutually exclusive in *Harlots*. Going back to Farley et al.'s question earlier, however, it is nonetheless implied that there is no "real alternative" for most of the women in this world, for although most of the sex on sale appears to be consensual, it is indeed coerced in that it is only conducted out of financial necessity. Most of the characters here are economically vulnerable, with no other means of "survival," and are perilously close to poverty and hunger. It could be argued, of course, that that is also true of all working-class characters in the show, who are all being exploited and coerced one way or another (even those like Amelia and her mother who see fit to judge and condemn sex work). But within these complex negotiations of consent and capitalism, the series' subplots focus on nonconsensual sex, which may be separate from the core business of the industry but shows its dark side, and this will be the subject of our next section.

SEXUAL VIOLENCE IN *HARLOTS*

Harlots reminds us that the world of prostitution is one in which violence, both sexual and physical, is never very far away. In the very first episode Kitty (Lottie Tolhurst) casually confides to Lucy that she became a prostitute after a friend of her father's "forced himself upon her"; abuse is regularly dealt out to Emily Lacey and the other girls at Quigley's at the hands of the sadistic client Mr. Osborne; all the prostitutes seem to be regularly assaulted in the street. In this, it seems, very little has changed. Farley et al. cite evidence proving that, today, rape is a constant reality for sex workers worldwide:

> Our findings from 9 countries on 5 continents indicate that the physical and emotional violence in prostitution is overwhelming ... 60 percent to 75 percent [of respondents] were raped in prostitution ... [but] it is likely that all of the estimates of violence reported here are conservative, and that the actual incidence of violence is greater than we found. (2003)

This is in contrast to an estimated 20 percent of women who experience sexual violence in the general population, although this is probably also a conservative estimate (Rape Crisis, 2021). We cannot extrapolate exact figures for the eighteenth-century setting of the show—rape was probably even more underreported by women then than now (Mills 141)—but Rubenhold suggests that it was, unsurprisingly, probably even more commonplace in the eighteenth century:

> A great number of the women who appear on *Harris's List* found their way into the sex trade on account of what would today be considered rape. If the picture presented by the *List* is to be believed, many also ended up in prostitution on account of child sexual abuse . . . women and girls from the lower ranks of society existed to be used by their social superiors . . . of course, in a system so stacked against them, few women of the lower and middling orders would have the resolve to bring these crimes to the notice of the authorities. (Rubenhold 2012: 2)

As with their real-life sources, no character in *Harlots* would consider involving the law, which they mostly fear or have amused contempt for (the local watchman, Armitage, is one of their customers) should they fall victim to this crime. That said, the show takes pains to ensure some rapists are punished one way or another, most dramatically in series 1 when Margaret Wells's elder daughter Charlotte is raped by her "keeper" Sir George Howard (Hugh Skinner), after she attempts to leave him (See figure 5.1).

This is a shocking plotline in many ways, partly because it is so unexpected. The first half of the series has constructed George as a figure of fun in his society: an ineffectual, rather stupid, aristocrat who is constantly laughed at by his friends because he is desperately in love with Charlotte, but constantly cuckolded and exploited by her. Hugh Skinner had previously played similar long-suffering, devoted but rather unintelligent lovers in British comedy

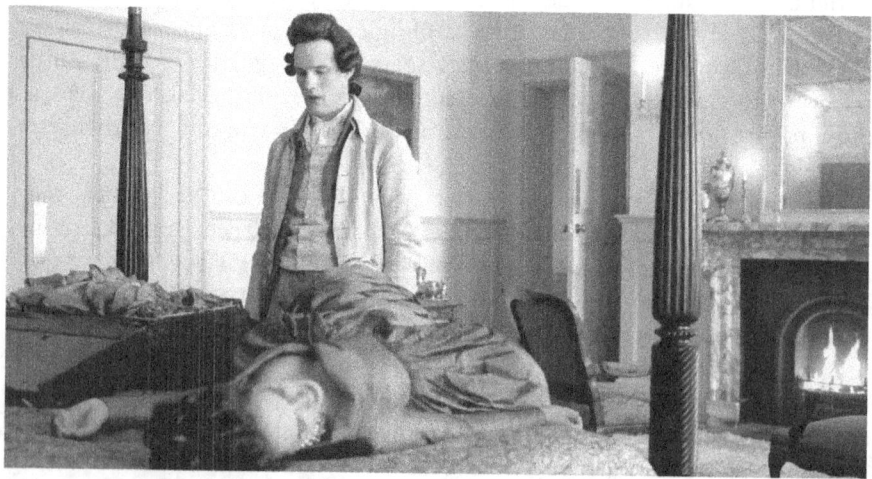

Figure 5.1 Charlotte's Keeper, Sir George, Turns Violent in *Harlots*, Episode 1:5 (2017).
Source: Screen grab by Katherine Byrne.

shows *Fleabag* and *W1A*, and is now instantly recognizable on British television as this kind of unthreatening character who an audience does not need to take too seriously. It is then all the more shocking when he forces himself on Charlotte, and afterward brings her to a society dinner, confident now that he has tamed her and that she "will now behave herself" (episode 6). The message is clear: even the most seemingly harmless men are capable of rape, given the motivation or opportunity, and this has of course been one of the recurrent themes explored by the shows we discuss throughout this book. *Harlots* reminds us, however, that money is the real enabler of the crime, for having once purchased Charlotte, George believes he has a perpetual right to her body. "Men of privilege . . . are taught to expect female compliance," as Dowd-Arrow and Creel put it (2016: 11). Money and class also ensure safety afterward: Sir George is exposed to his friends as a rapist, and is condemned by them verbally, but there is no question that he will be formally charged or imprisoned for an attack on a whore. The series ensures some form of internal justice, however, for, in an unusual example of female characters in a period drama taking revenge (albeit indirectly) for rape, George is soon punished for what he has done. Emboldened by his first rape, he tries next to purchase and then immediately attack Charlotte's younger sister Lucy and is stabbed by her in self-defense. As he bleeds out, Margaret Wells hastens his end to protect her daughter, and soon all her girls and the whole household are complicit in the murder of a "cull" for whom they clearly feel no sympathy. Because of Sir George's social position, though, no one turns a blind eye to this crime, in contrast to those perpetuated on female characters, and there is an investigation. With a nice symmetry, however, Justice Cunliffe, the representative of the law who learns the truth, is himself fatally stabbed because of his involvement in procuring girls for others to rape. In this world, most people are corrupt, and anyone can be a villain, especially the rich and powerful who have the means to cover up their crimes.

If this plotline reveals that any man can be a rapist, it also reveals that any woman can be a victim. If Charlotte, the "most beautiful whore in London," sought after and with powerful friends, can be raped in what was her own bedroom, no woman is safe from this crime. This is echoed by a plotline in series 2 when we learn that George's widow, now the wealthy Lady Isabella, was once raped by her own brother. Privilege is not necessarily a guarantee of safety from sexual violence. It is, however, most often the poor and socially vulnerable girls who are the targets of male brutality in the show, and its most disturbing representation of rape for sale addresses this. With what seems to be recent events like the Epstein case in mind, the darkest plotline in the show—and one that continues into series 2—concerns the purchase of a supply of young virgins for a group of powerful men, significantly with the assistance of both madams. From the first episode, *Harlots* reminds us that virginity was a commodity prized above all else in this society—sadly with great historical accuracy:

> The age set [in the eighteenth century] for Statutory Rape (under ten) created a distinction between women, available for sex, and children, not available for sex. This was itself problematic as the erotic fascination with virginity and defloration had a powerful hold over the eighteenth-century imagination. To desire to have sexual intercourse with very young girls was entirely within the boundaries of acceptable sexual behaviour. (Mills, 141)

Virginity does not occupy quite the same place in the mainstream cultural imagination today, but this plotline makes us reflect uncomfortably that youth and innocence still does. It is now problematic to openly desire a child, but not an older teenager, despite a huge age gap, and the Epstein case revealed how lucrative it might be to secure a supply of such girls for the rich and powerful. Margaret Wells is preparing to exploit the eighteenth-century "erotic fascination with virginity" through her youngest daughter, fifteen-year-old Lucy, who lives in her mother's brothel but has been kept untouched in order to make substantial money when she is launched into the market.

Lucy is Wells's favorite child, but her sentimentalism only extends to waiting three more years before entering the profession than she had allowed her sister Charlotte. Episode 1 ends with the auctioning of her virginity, with bids submitted by older, predatory men. Tim McInnerny is particularly sinister as Lord Repton, who wishes with disturbing relish to deflower Lucy as he had done her sister Charlotte years before. When Lucy is finally sent to him for this purpose, she is placed in a position which sums up the intersecting problems of prostitution and consent. Removed from the relative safety of London and driven by carriage to Repton's country home, she becomes frightened—correctly as it turns out, for he is a sadist—and tries to renege on the deal, but soon realizes that freedom of choice is not a luxury enjoyed by her profession, marginalized and unprotected under the law as it is:

Lucy: "Stop do you hear me! I want you to stop! I wasn't told we'd be leaving London. If you don't take me home I will get out and walk."
Coachman: "And become the plunder of footpads? It won't be just your purse they shove their fingers in."
Lucy: "I want to go home."
Coachman: "I will take you. But you will have to make good with me . . . you can take me in your mouth if you prefer."
Lucy: "I'm a guest of your master."
Coachman: "You are not his guest, you are his doxy. And you won't even be that once you've jilted him." (episode 3)

Rape by someone seems inevitable for a prostitute in this situation, and Lucy goes ahead with her assignation, rationalizing that at least she—or rather her mother—will be well paid to be raped by Repton. We could consider this scene an appeal for the regulation and legalization of the profession: Lucy is willing to provide sexual services, but wishes to do so on her own terms, in a safe way. Instead, she is afterward physically and mentally scarred by the experience, arguably as much a victim of her society's lack of concern for her as she is of Repton's sadism.

Nonetheless, Lucy still can be considered lucky compared with the victims of the other main rape plotline in the series, who meet a much worse fate. These girls are virgins tricked and then imprisoned by Lydia Quigley to meet the demands of an unknown group of men, known as "the Spartans," who are only interested in abusing the young and innocent, and who pay well for the privilege. Quigley finds the undertaking "vile"—and, rarely for her, even appears to feel guilty about it—but carries out the procurement anyway, because she knows it is for rich, "formidably powerful" members of the upper classes (episode 5). The audience only sees the events through her eyes: the selection of suitably innocent, job-seeking girls she pretends to have a respectable job for, and then a brief scene where one traumatized, sobbing victim is sold on to another brothel, now "ruined" but no longer useful. The second victim disappears and has presumably met a terrible, violent end, and even Quigley is moved to something like concern at this: "Where's the girl? I found blood, what have you done to her?" (episode 5). Far from being satisfied, the appetites of those who have bought her seem to only grow in sadism and cruelty as they are indulged: as Justice Cunliffe puts it, "We need another girl. It is a growing beast that must be fed." Indeed, Quigley too becomes increasingly unconcerned with morality or guilt, and continues to facilitate this kind of procurement well into the next series, alongside the brothel that constitutes her core business.

Rape for profit here, then, is not an individual crime but a many layered system of abuse that involves Quigley and Cunliffe as procurers, other pimps as accessories after the fact, the law as protector of crime, a hidden community of men as consumers, and underpinning it all a wider social system which renders women economically insecure and hence vulnerable to abuse. All of this seems far from remote from our own society. Conversations between Quigley and Cunliffe in which she assures him that she has chosen well and "no-one will come looking for these girls" bears a chilling similarity to what the press has reported about Epstein's victims today:

> We live in a sexualized culture, one that relentlessly demeans women starting in their tween years. While no woman, young or old, is safe from this, it must be said that class distinctions apply here too. The young, the powerless and the

poverty-struck are even more vulnerable to the powerful and wealthy. Epstein, a practiced predator, apparently knew this. He and his helpers seemed to specialize in targeting girls from working-class homes with absentee or overwhelmed parents. . . . It's hard not to suspect that if Epstein was preying on the daughters of the well-connected, he would have done more serious jail time when originally charged. (Olen 2019)

Similar accusations have been levied at American singer R. Kelly, whose case is currently being tried, and who allegedly also exploited society's racism by preying on young black girls who the system would not care enough about to investigate. No parents or guardians make inquiries about the abductees in *Harlots*, who, because they are all poor and working class, become lost girls in eighteenth-century London. It is only Margaret Wells, the matriarch and in most ways the heroine of the show, who cares enough about the abductions to report the conspiracy to the law. Wells, we learn in the final episode, had long committed to support other women and to provide a safe place for them to work. She, too, however, is tempted by Justice Cunliffe to become involved in this procurement to save her own skin (as he knows she has murdered Sir George), and it is only at the last minute that she cannot go through with his plan to drug and hand over Amelia to the Spartans. Wells's struggle between self-preservation and her own moral code reminds the viewer of the pervasive ways in which power can blackmail and manipulate even fundamentally good people for its own ends. And ultimately, of course, her intervention only works on a small scale: Amelia is saved, but after the murder of Cunliffe, Quigley is safe, the other perpetrators remain unknown, and the pursuit of innocent girls continues into series 2.

CONCLUSION

Harlots is one of the few shows on television to represent prostitution in a nuanced, unerotic, and uncliched way. In its often-positive, even humorous view of the "oldest profession" (here represented as a supportive community of women living and working together in the Wells's house), it reflects the views of sex-positive feminists, that prostitution is no worse a job for women than much other paid labor. Similarly, in its frequent reminders that the law fails to protect these women, it seems to suggest that this profession should be socially and legally sanctioned. However, it also reminds the viewer that the sex trade does not deal with exclusively consenting adults. Through its depiction of the rape culture so pervasive in eighteenth-century society, and the willingness of mercenary Madams like Lydia Quigley to facilitate it, the show creates uncomfortable parallels with the trafficking that takes place in our own society. In particular, its cynical representation of wealth and privilege reveals how closely they can be aligned with networks of sexual abuse. This anxiety about the establishment is shared by other gritty period dramas set in preindustrial London, *Taboo* (BBC, 2017–) and *The Frankenstein Chronicles* (2015–2017). The former critiques the dark past of the East India Company, and the latter explores the potential for corruption inherent in the medical profession, as Byrne has discussed elsewhere (Byrne, 2018). It is apparent that, in the last few years, period shows about the British urban past have reflected what Krakauer, writing about Epstein, has identified as a "growing distrust with all forms of power" (2019) which has often been brought about by the exposure of scandals involving the concealment of rape and other sexual violence. From long-hidden child abuse by the Catholic church to the covering up of decades-long crimes by BBC presenter and "philanthropist" Jimmy Savile (Halliday 2014), Harvey Weinstein, and Jeffrey Epstein, our society is increasingly aware that power buys silence, facilitating crime and allowing it to be concealed, and that things need to change:

> The downfall of Epstein is great news for his victims who were denied justice the first time around. But it's also the latest example of a recent, broader phenomenon—the crumbling of the elites. . . . A 2017 poll by The Associated Press found an astoundingly high 82 percent of Americans say they think "wealthy people" have too much power and influence in Washington. (Krakauer 2019)

This is of course not just an American phenomenon: distrust of "elites" of all kinds in Britain has also escalated, and has been blamed for events like Brexit, which has been considered the manifestation of a growing populism among British people. Significantly, the BBC itself has come under attack in this regard, its reputation tarnished because of possible concealment of the Savile case (he was one of the main presenters of the highly popular British show *Top of The Pops* for some seventeen years, during which time he and another DJ abused dozens of children), and its credibility because of alleged biased reporting of recent political issues (Davies, 2018). It is tempting to see its recent purchase—from ITV Encore—of *Harlots* as part of an effort to redress its perceived failings (it is also currently broadcasting *I Will Destroy You*, a contemporary show which also features rape and its cover-ups as its main subject matter). At any rate, while *Harlots* feels like an edgy choice, it is not because it is the "bawdiest the BBC have ever aired" but because it is so irreverent and cynical about society. This world seems to be part of a quite distant past—preindustrial, pre-sanitation, grimy and gritty—but its numerous rape plotlines act as a reminder of the links between power, authority, and abuse, and reveal that, in this regard, our present has evolved very little.

Chapter 6

"If You Can't Rape Your Wife, Who Can You Rape?"

Marital Rape in The Forsyte Saga *and* Poldark

In 1987, Susan Estrich's book *Real Rape* drew much-needed attention to the narrow legal and social interpretation of rape in the United States that had persisted since the previous century. Traditionally, the law refused to consider "simple rape," in which the assailant is unarmed and known to the victim, as being on a par with "real rape," that is, stranger rape with a weapon. Of these supposedly less serious versions of the crime, marital rape, Estrich argued, is the most "extreme" example and the most problematic under the law:

> The continued force of the marital exemption is a product of the very same notions . . . that have made marital rapes difficult to prosecute: notions of presumed consent, made absolute, views of "appropriate relationships" as private, and sex within those relationships as ambiguous and subject to continuous readjustment, judgments that betrayal by an intimate is not a serious harm. (Estrich, 1987: 74)[1]

As a result, "rape within marriage is the most common and most frequently excused form of sexual violation," and the most sanctioned by popular culture, as the famously romanticized rape of Scarlett O'Hara in *Gone with the Wind* in the 1930s displayed (Bourke, 306). While "based on a true story" TV movies like *The Burning Bed* (starring Farrah Fawcett; 1984) exposed domestic and sexual violence in marriage, more widely viewed soap operas like *Dynasty* in the 1980s still trivialized marital rape as the result of a husband's sexual frustration, and which roses the following day could amend. The old idea that it was a husband's conjugal right to have sex with his wife, and that a marriage contract meant permanent consent, was, shockingly, held up in law in Britain and the United States until the 1990s, with husbands exempt from prosecution until this time. Even after this point, this type of rape remains "the most difficult form of abuse to successfully prosecute," and yet it is likely to be the most common form of rape: "Among ever-married women, husband-/ex-husband perpetrated rape was four times more common than stranger-perpetrated rape" (Mahoney and Williams, 1998: 2). Despite this, however, different, less severe punishment for marital rape continues into the twenty-first century.

Much has changed since the publication of Estrich's book and now most, though by no means all, of the countries of the world regard rape within marriage as a crime.[2] It still remains a gray area for the public, however, even in the UK: as *The Guardian* observes, as late as 2018 "almost a quarter of the 4,000 people questioned in the Attitudes to Sexual Consent survey carried out by YouGov believed sex without consent in long-term relationships was usually not rape" (Topping 2018). This ambiguity among Western society is reflected in the fan responses to some of the period dramas we examine in this chapter, which, from the 1960s onward, have played a significant role in raising awareness about marital rape.

As this book has proved is so often the case, period drama television leads the way in the representation of marital rape. From the famous rape in one of the most watched shows of all time, *The Forsyte Saga* (1967), right up to the present day with the recent adaptation of Elena Ferrante's novel trilogy, *My Brilliant Friend* (2018), period television has reminded us that marital rape is indeed "real" and deserves representation on our small screens, whether it is only alluded to or shown in more brutal detail. In the 1974 BBC adaptation of Anthony Trollope's Victorian novel *Phineas Finn*, for example, Lady Laura's husband politely warns her, over tea, that he "shall claim his legal rights" even if she does not love him. It is a far less violent scene than the more recent image of sixteen-year-old Lila (Gaia Girace) in *My Brilliant Friend* being beaten for refusing her husband (played by Giovanni Amura) on their wedding night. The camera focuses on Lila's face and small foot crushed under Stefano's heavy body. Both series, filmed over four decades apart about women in different countries and different centuries, underscore how universal this experience is. In *My Brilliant Friend*, the brutishness of the perpetrator, played by an equally unattractive actor, reinforces for the viewer the seriousness of marital rape and the long-term trauma of its victims. Lila's husband, previously shown gorging himself on food and drink at their wedding banquet, is equally savage in bed. Another series, *Outlander*, which has never shied away from showing sexual violence, only shows us the physical results of marital rape, rather than the act itself, when Claire treats the fractured wrist of gang leader Lionel Brown's wife, Rose, who confides that her husband hurt her because she refused "to lie with him" (episode 5:11). In response to Rose's declarations of self-blame,

Claire tells her that "a good man wouldn't hurt you"—similar words that *Poldark*'s Dr. Dwight Enys will use to remind Ossie Whitworth to treat his wife Morwenna "with kindness" rather than asserting his "rights" by force in the bedroom. While all of the women in these examples are clearly victims, there are, disturbingly, some instances in which the depiction of marital rape elicits more sympathy from viewers for the husband than the wife, as the case of not just one but two TV adaptations of John Galsworthy's Edwardian novel, *The Forsyte Saga*, illustrate. This chapter will focus on marital rape committed by husbands against wives, but as we discussed in our earlier chapter on male rape, in *Bridgerton* there is the rare but significant example of "a dubious consent encounter" (Prescott 2020) in which the husband is a victim.

MARITAL RAPE AND HISTORY: *THE DUCHESS* (2008)

Writing about *The Duchess*, Saul Dibb's 2008 biopic of the Duchess of Devonshire, Jessica Taylor observes how marital rape is used as a device in what she identifies as "post-feminist historical chick-flicks" (Taylor 2016: 336). Dibb's film explores the oppression of the eighteenth-century woman, and, despite her wealth and privilege, her sexual and economic vulnerability under the laws of the time. In this film, the central character "Gee" (played by Keira Knightley) is unhappily married and has to accept her husband's repeated adultery but is not permitted her own love affair. When she tries to assert her rights, she is raped by her husband (played by Ralph Fiennes) in order to put her in her place—"Stay here and do what I say," he tells her afterward—and to force her to fulfill her main job, the production of a male heir (Dibbs, 2008). This rape acts, Taylor argues, as a "shorthand to indicate the female body's subjection to institutionally supported forms of punishment" (Taylor, 2016: 337). Like the other rapes we explore in this chapter, the lack of consent is never in doubt: we see Gee running away from her husband and saying "no" repeatedly as he throws her violently onto the bed. The rape itself takes place mostly off camera but is still a highly painful experience for the audience: they, like several horrified household members who are nearby, overhear Gee's continuing screams but are powerless to intervene. As a result, the attack provokes a feeling of outrage in a contemporary viewer, especially because it is also overheard by one of Gee's children (as many real-life marital rapes are reported to be: see Mahoney and Williams, 1998: 24). It is only one of many ways in which Gee, and indeed all the women in the film, are exploited and abused by patriarchy, and this provokes a feminist response in the viewer. However, because marital rape is now illegal, this film invites us to judge the past for its shortcomings, while being thankful for our present:

This historicized trope of legal marital rape thus stands in opposition to an allegedly more enlightened and equal postfeminist present, and thus obscures the ways that marital rape, and rape more broadly, continue to occur across the world. . . . [Historical film] arguably allows the postfeminist audience to openly and positively explore feminist issues without threatening the status quo of the cultural context in which such films were produced. (Taylor, 2016: 342)

Condemning the prefeminist past, Taylor argues, blinds us to the many problems for women in the twenty-first century, including, of course, the continuing reality of sexual violence from a spouse. This is an important framework through which to consider the rapes explored in this chapter. They, like the rape of Gee, are all presented as attempts by men to assert or take back control over their wives and invite thankfulness in their audiences that such crimes are no longer legally sanctioned. Never has period drama been more "anti-nostalgic" than when it represents marital rape: as with *The Duchess*, these shows take pains to bring home the horror of violent betrayal by someone you live with, someone you should be able to trust, and who legally has power over you. Yet any sense of smugness about our more "enlightened and equal" present should evaporate when we consider the other threats to feminism displayed by these plotlines. For example, marital rape is frequently less important than, and gives way to, a romance plot: Morwenna in the most recent adaptation of *Poldark* may take longer than Gee to be "cured" of her unhappiness by a handsome young lover, but cured she is, to the delight of fans who are more invested in their reunion than they are in her recovery. But Morwenna and Gee have at least both benefited from increasing support for feminism as a result of the fourth wave: prior to this, Irene in *The Forsyte Saga* (1967; 2002) is presented and judged much more harshly, as we will now discuss.

"SHE HAD IT COMING TO HER": *THE FORSYTE SAGA*

Fifty years ago, viewers jammed the BBC switchboard with complaints that the marital rape scene in the televised adaptation of *The Forsyte Saga* (1967) was too indecent for a Sunday night audience. In just thirty seconds, an enraged Soames Forsyte (Eric Porter) chases his unfaithful wife Irene (Nyree Dawn Porter) upstairs, throws her on the bed, shreds her dress to partially reveal her heaving breasts, and yells, "Anyone can have you, can't they—well, I can too," as the camera pans to the organ grinder outside their London town house. The first modern TV costume drama, *The Forsyte Saga* sparked a national debate in Britain; while viewers at the time complained that the realism of the scene was inappropriate for a Sunday night, they ultimately felt little sympathy for Irene and were quick to forgive, or even condone, her husband's actions. In *Edwardians on Screen*, Byrne describes the rape of Irene as "one of the most famous rapes in television history" and yet notes that "the discourse it provokes is startlingly antifeminist" (Byrne, 2015: 48). The perceived immorality of Irene, who Soames suspects of infidelity, apparently turned viewers against her. As discussed in the introduction to this chapter, marital rape has long seemed like a special case: not so much an act of violence as a part of the complicated relations of a marriage. Hence the state and society as a whole have long been wary of becoming involved in what happens between couples, in the home. Similarly, viewers seemed reluctant to judge a man for taking by force what the law had long said was his—especially when another man had tried to steal it. Soames's actions are mitigated here by implication that as Irene has herself broken the marriage contract through her adultery, she deserves to be "reprimanded" by rape. And in 1967, with second-wave feminism still in its early days, this adaptation of an Edwardian novel, set in the 1880s, did not seem so out of sync with the times. The television review program, *Late Night Line-Up*, at the time conducted a poll of viewers asking who was "in the right"—with only 39% of respondents siding with Irene (Bignell, 2003: 236).

This public reaction to the Forsyte rape was likely encouraged further by the casting of Eric Porter, a charismatic actor already well-known as a Shakespearean leading man, as Soames. Unfortunately, popular culture has long promoted the myth that men we know, who are good-looking and heroic in other ways, are in fact incapable of sexual violence. Media critic Clementine Ford (2016) has chastised period dramas, whose popularity banks on handsome leading men, for feeding into the "real rape" myth by keeping alive the dangerous notion that "rapists can only be loud, dirty, outsider criminal men." Instead, as Ford notes, "Exploring the complexities of when two versions of the same man present themselves would make for much more interesting television." And even in the twenty-first century, fans continue to be complicit in this conflation of the actor/hero: in a 2016 Amazon review for the DVD copy of the 1967 adaptation, one such viewer enthused, "As the central character, Soames Forsyte, the chiseled Eric Porter is watchable, complicated—and if not sympathetic—always understandable even at his most bestial" (McKee 2016).

Such comments underscore how the experience of marital rape in the twenty-first century still remains, as Bennice and Resick argue, "invalidated for its victims, legally, culturally and professionally" (2003: 228). This can be seen very clearly in the 2002 Granada TV adaptation of *The Forsyte Saga* as once again an adaptation prioritizes Soames's point of view rather than that of his victim. Actor Damian Lewis was already on his way to becoming a British heartthrob, but his performance as Soames in 2002 would seal his reputation as "the thinking woman's pin-up" (Byrne 2015: 47). He did, however, have some initial reservations about playing the part of a spousal rapist. Referring to that decisive moment in the story, he expected viewers would be troubled as to how they reacted to his character, "thinking, God I feel sorry for Soames, but he just raped his wife!" (Byrne 2015: 45).

Galsworthy's novel gives no details of that night, only this comment the next day: "The morning after a certain night on which Soames had at last asserted his rights and acted like a man, he breakfasted alone" (Galsworthy 2008: 264). Both TV adaptations, therefore, imagined for viewers what that scene would look like, and both scenes overwhelmingly elicited sympathy for the perpetrator, not the victim, of sexual violence. Unlike the 1967 version which does not show us the rape once Soames throws Irene on to the bed, the 2002 adaptation gives us three minutes and fifteen seconds, during which time Soames clamps his hand over his wife's mouth, telling her, "Lie still, I say. Be quiet . . . be nice to me for once." The rape is admittedly not eroticized, and we might expect such a long scene to bring home the horror of the crime (see figure 6.1). And yet, as Byrne notes, the TV writers were determined to make Soames "sympathetic" in the buildup to and aftermath of the rape, reasoning that viewers would "get over" their conflicted feelings: "You do end up loving him . . . [but] he's a rapist! But you can understand what's driven him to it"—and what's "driven him to it" is the "coldness" and adulterous actions of Irene (Byrne 2015: 45). TV critic Elizabeth Grice, writing for *The Telegraph* the morning after this scene aired, agreed that the "iciness" of Irene, as played by Gina McKee, most likely made viewers feel that "she had it coming to her." Even more troubling is Grice's comment that the rape must be "the talk of the canteens this morning" since, her review

Figure 6.1 Soames and Irene and Marital Rape in *The Forsyte Saga*, Episode 4 (2002).
Source: Screen grab by Julie Anne Taddeo.

continued, viewers surely wondered before the episode aired how "Damian Lewis as Soames would *ravish* his icy spouse" (Grice 2002, emphasis added).

The repeated use of "icy" to describe Irene is significant. We would expect the gains of second-wave feminism and the success of the anti-rape movement to have changed attitudes to marital rape dramatically in the thirty-five years between these two adaptations. Instead, we see marital rape still being justified, this time via a postfeminist emphasis on female sexual availability: part of what Ariel Levy would term the rise of "raunch culture" in her 2005 book *Female Chauvinist Pigs*:

> We have determined that all empowered women must be overtly and publicly sexual . . . for women, and only for women, hotness requires projecting a kind of eagerness, offering a promise that any attention you receive for your physicality is welcome. . . . Proving that you are worthy of lust and necessarily—that you seek to provoke lust is still exclusively women's work. (Levy, 2005: 33)

For Irene, this includes the "attention" of a husband she no longer loves or desires. She gets no sympathy from viewers in 2002, because they are the product of a culture which assumes being sexually "free" and participating in their own objectification is part of being a woman. Clearly, the rape victim cannot win: where in the 1960s the character deserved to be raped because she adulterously betrayed her husband, now she deserves it because she is frigid toward him.

The continuing anti-feminist response to Irene—from TV critics and viewers alike (some of whom have conducted such informal online polls as "Irene: Beautiful Victim or Ugly Bitch?" [The Straight Dope Message Board, 2017])—is indeed troubling. What is lost in both adaptations and fan responses is what Helen Goodman argues is Galsworthy's critique of Victorian and Edwardian attitudes about marital rape: that although he fails to offer us Irene's point of view in the novel, Galsworthy *does* consider Soames "in the wrong" and his actions unforgiveable (Goodman, 2012: 51). In the novel, Soames tries to rationalize his actions as his right over his wife's body which the law at the time acknowledged as his "property" (the subheading of the novel is, after all, *The Man of Property*); nevertheless, he is haunted by the memory of Irene's "terrible smothered sobbing, the like of which he had never heard, and still seemed to hear" and for which he felt an "intolerable feeling of remorse and shame"(Galsworthy, 2008: 252). While we might expect that a twenty-first-century adaptation for TV would imagine how Irene reacts to the rape, we still only witness Soames's "remorse and shame," *his* post-rape breakdown. Excuses are even made for Soames's actions in the TV version by his mother who observes that her son "feel[s] things too much." We earlier explored television's prioritizing of the male experience of rape over the victim's—even when he is the perpetrator—in more detail in chapter 2. In this case, however, the conflation of the character and the "chiseled" actors playing him in 1967 or 2002 seems to explain viewers' willingness to forgive—and certainly are not unique to *The Forsyte Saga*. In our next case study, with a less attractive marital rapist, the "marriage assumes consent" defense seems less justifiable to viewers—although we might also hope that the increasing awareness that accompanied #MeToo in the interval makes it now less acceptable to "forgive" these kinds of husbands.

"LIVING WITH HER RAPIST": MARITAL RAPE IN *POLDARK*

The attractiveness of the male lead, along with judgment of the sexuality of the female victim, in *The Forsyte Saga* explains in part viewers' willingness to justify or forgive acts of sexual violence against women, and we see the same response to the rape committed by Ross Poldark as discussed in our first chapter. In stark contrast, the actions of the Reverend Ossie Whitworth (Christian Brassington), who repeatedly rapes his young bride Morwenna Chynoweth (Ellise Chappell), during seasons 3 and 4 of *Poldark* (aired in 2017–2018), prompt only horror and disgust from viewers. Actress Ellise Chappell noted in an interview that fans told her Morwenna's story "touched them" (Cannon 2019) and yet, Morwenna's case is an example where some victims are prioritized over others. No one on social media has ever accused Morwenna of deserving her fate at the hands of the odious Ossie, and yet, Irene Forsyte too was forced into a mercenary marriage for the sake of her mother. Had viewers been shown the impact of Soames's actions on her emotional state, perhaps viewers would not still be debating if Irene "had it coming to her."

We have written elsewhere about Morwenna's story line as it was represented in the 1975–1977 adaptation of *Poldark* (Taddeo 2014), but there is surprisingly very little difference between the first TV adaptation and the more recent one filmed forty years later. *Poldark*'s creator, Winston Graham, had earlier explored marital rape in his novel *Marnie* (1961) and he clearly took pains to bring home the horror of marital rape in both his *Poldark* novels and the 1970s' TV adaptation in which he had a hands-on role as adviser.[3] Graham resumed writing his *Poldark* series of novels in the early 1970s, just as the first season of the BBC adaptation (based on the novels written between 1945 and 1953) was being filmed, and so he clearly made a conscious choice to address marital rape in great detail. He added the character, Morwenna Chynoweth, yet another impoverished but genteel member of Elizabeth's family, whose arranged marriage to Reverend Whitworth ("Ossie") in *The*

Black Moon (1973) and the ensuing abuse she endures in *The Four Swans* (1976) became a major plot point of the second season of *Poldark* in 1977. Written when domestic violence and rape took center stage in the feminist movement—Brownmiller's book was published the year before *The Four Swans*—Graham's novels suggest the timelessness of these issues (for Morwenna in the late eighteenth century and for his readers and TV audience almost 200 years later); he also focused as much on the psychological as the physical damage caused by rape. The first of many instances of marital rape occurs on Morwenna's wedding night:

> Once she resisted and once he hit her, but after that she made no protest. So eventually he laid her naked on the bed, where she curled up like a frightened snail. Then he knelt at the side of the bed and said a short prayer before he got up and began to tickle her bare feet before he raped her. (Graham 1973: 532)

In the 1977 TV adaptation, viewers are not privy to this wedding night rape; such scenes were perhaps too explicit for a costume drama in which clothes remained on and hair and makeup untouched even during the most intimate encounters (as attested by Elizabeth's [Jill Townsend] perfectly coiffed appearance in season 1's bedroom scene with Ross [Robin Ellis] in 1975). The BBC's 1967 production of *The Forsyte Saga* had already scandalized audiences with its scene of Soames ripping Irene's bodice, implying the marital rape that would follow. But it is obvious from Morwenna's stunned face and revulsion after Ossie rolls off her during their only filmed sexual encounter in a later episode that she is not a consenting participant.

Graham perhaps introduced this story line not just to comment on women's oppression in the past but as a vehicle for contemporary legal and social change in the 1970s. When warned by Morwenna's physician that his nightly sexual demands threaten the health of his wife and unborn child, Ossie (in both the novel and TV versions) roars that it is the legal and moral duty of a wife to submit. Here he is echoing, almost verbatim, the oft-cited statement by Justice Sir Matthew Hale that remained in effect until 1991 when the marital rape exemption was at last overturned by English courts: "But the husband cannot be guilty of rape committed by himself upon his lawful wife, for by their mutual matrimonial consent and contract, the wife hath given up herself in this kind unto her husband which she cannot retract." Graham was ahead of his time, and the legal system, by rejecting this judgment.

By the time the latest BBC adaptation of *Poldark* revisited this plotline in 2017 (See figure 6.2), it was possible to be more explicit, and also more knowing, about the wider social circumstances that condone or facilitate rape. This newer version also draws more intently on Graham's criticism of religion, which Ossie has used to excuse his actions: as Ossie unbuckles his

Figure 6.2 Ossie and Morwenna and Marital Rape in *Poldark*, Episode 3:8 (2017).
Source: Screen grab by Julie Anne Taddeo.

belt and approaches a terrified Morwenna, he tells her, "In the words of Saint Paul, wives submit yourselves unto your husbands as onto your lord," and then insists they "say a little prayer" as the screen fades out (episode 4:5). Although Ossie is the perpetrator of this crime, this twenty-first-century adaptation also shows how a number of other characters have colluded in it. George Warleggan (Jack Farthing), for example, makes it clear that he is willing to prostitute Morwenna for the connections a marriage to Ossie would bring him (he essentially blackmails her by threatening Drake Carne, with whom she's in love, with prison and execution for a crime he didn't commit): "What, I wonder, would you stake to see him (Drake) acquitted?" (episode 3:6) he asks his wife's frightened cousin. Elizabeth (Heida Reed) is also complicit, having encouraged her cousin's marriage to Ossie: both Warleggans consider it a way to indirectly punish Ross through his family connection with Drake (Harry Richardson). After Ossie's fortuitous death in season 4, Morwenna at last reveals to the Warleggans what their handiwork has done to her: at Ossie's funeral, Elizabeth and George express their condolences, but Morwenna reprimands them for forcing her into a marriage that was "advantageous" to them but resulted in her being "violated . . . again and again and again." Even Dr. Enys (Luke Norris), although he did his best to intervene after the birth of Morwenna's child, is ultimately silenced and allowed the abuse to continue. Most of the rapes committed by Ossie occurred during season 3 which aired in 2017—still prior to #MeToo, though only by a few months—but this plotline shows an increasing awareness, reflected in that movement, that society as a whole is complicit in rape, a theme explored in *Outlander* a year later, as we discussed earlier in the case of Brianna's rape. And, with the family pressures placed on Morwenna, the ever-enduring socioeconomic causes of marital rape are also alluded to here. Ossie repeatedly threatens Morwenna with institutionalization in an asylum if she did not "submit," just as, in *The Duchess*, the Duke threatens Gee with the loss of her children and buys her silence with his wealth: timely reminders of the legal and financial realities that compelled, and still compel, so many women to endure marital rape.

Notably, as with *The Duchess* but unlike the earlier dramas that deal with this subject matter, there is no downplaying here of the horrors of marital rape in the most recent *Poldark* adaptation. Ossie frequently threatens Morwenna with physical violence; she looks terrified whenever he is near, cowering in bed on more than one occasion and clearly in pain from the previous night when he forces himself on her again the next day. Such scenes, and the ongoing nature of this rape plot (which continues well into season 4), do bring home to the viewer Mahoney and Williams's observation (paraphrasing Finkelhor and Yllo, 1983) that "a woman who is raped by a stranger lives with a memory of a horrible attack; a woman who is raped by her husband lives with her rapist" (1998: 3).

Some of these scenes involving Ossie and Morwenna did in fact prompt viewer complaints to the BBC. In response to these complaints, the UK's Rape Crisis Center spokesperson Katie Russell described the marital rape scenes in *Poldark* as "harrowing" but necessary rather than gratuitous in that they drew attention to the horrors of (at the time) legally sanctioned sexual violence (Debnath 2017). Presumably, *Poldark*'s production company, Mammoth Screen, had learnt lessons from their controversial "bedroom encounter" between Ross and Elizabeth the year before, and hence they wished this to be a much more disturbing "real rape." Significantly, Russell compared the two rape plots, noting that this one is "a lot less ambiguous (although both women explicitly cry 'no'), so I think in that way it's quite positive . . . it is key not to portray those kind of scenes as titillation, sexualising or glamorising in any way [*sic*]" (Debnath 2017). This was, of course, what had happened with the previous rape plotline, which so many viewers did indeed consider "titillation," as we have discussed in chapter 1. But Russell also highlighted, unwittingly, the ways in which *Poldark*'s marital rape plot perpetuates old myths about rapists: "He's (Ossie) very clearly a bad man and so there's a very clear connection between his general unpleasantness, nastiness, misogyny and then the rape that he perpetrates against a very sympathetic and vulnerable character" (Debnath 217). Ossie as a "generally unpleasant" character is easier to accept as a rapist than Ross, and this is one of the reasons why viewers are more sympathetic to Morwenna than Elizabeth. When he is not raping his wife, Ossie is shown sucking the toes of prostitutes or his wife's younger sister, Rowella, as well as nearly bursting the buttons of his frivolous waistcoats (though a man of the cloth, he is gluttonous in his appetites: even Dr. Enys politely references his size, in urging him to forgo relations during

Morwenna's pregnancy). The contrast with handsome, "heroic" Ross is made clear, and so in some ways this plotline feels like the show's defense of the previous one. When riding in a carriage together in season 4, episode 3, we see these two men up close, and Ross is disgusted by Ossie's greed and lack of empathy when they discuss the poverty of his subordinate, the Reverend Odgers. The difference in compassion and care (and physical looks) between the two is striking. Even the ambiguous language Graham applied to Ross's encounter with Elizabeth in the novel version is discarded when describing Morwenna and Ossie's—specifically using the word "rape."

Ossie's presence in *Poldark* is not only to remind us that the past was open to abuse, then; his purpose is also to make Ross's actions insignificant by comparison. More disturbingly still, in the view of some critics, it is also to add humor to the show:

> In the book of Stuff That Shouldn't Need Explaining Nowadays But Somehow Still Does . . . there's an entry entitled Rape: Comedy. . . . It's nuanced stuff but concludes with an evergreen reminder: "Making rape the punchline to a seaside-postcard comedy skit is crass and cheap. Sheesh, c'mon, man. Why wouldn't you get that?" If said book weren't fictional, I'd send a copy to Poldark's creators. After a slathering Rev. Whitworth comically huffed and puffed his way to a convalescent Morwenna's bed, ignored her pleas of no and forced her to "submit," they're obviously due a reminder. Playing rape for laughs is a dick move. (Mellor 2017)

It is true that Ossie, a vicar, is a buffoon constantly at the mercy of his libido, and some scenes (like those with his—very young—sister-in-law) have a touch of the *Carry On* film about them. *Poldark* seems perpetually unsure how to manage the tone of its rape representations, lapsing constantly into the genres of 1970s pornography, bedroom farce, or romance. Indeed, given that Morwenna's rape is soon overshadowed by reconciliation with her true love Drake (and her suffering soon seems to be as much about pining for him as it is about her repeated attacks), this plotline combines all three, rather than being actually what it should be—tragedy.

Of course, romance is what most viewers are really looking for in *Poldark*. In both the twentieth- and twenty-first-century TV adaptations, Drake and Morwenna have rivaled Ross and Demelza as fans' "favorite couple" but despite their wedding and kiss which concluded season 2 in 1977, fans were left to wonder if the couple "would ever have a happy ending." When Graham revisited their marriage in the novel *The Loving Cup* (1984), Morwenna, though now approaching middle age and outwardly a happy wife and mother, still suffers nightmares from her treatment by her first husband, but she and Drake then disappear as characters while Graham focused on the next generation of Poldark children in later novels. Most adaptations typically would follow the source text in this way, for it is rare for a TV drama to delve deeply into the lingering effects of rape trauma. Anna Bates in *Downton Abbey* insists she wants to put the episode behind her, and she does; *A Place to Call Home*'s Carolyn Bligh, after her rapist is beaten by her husband, never mentions her own assault again; Irene Forsyte's is simply ignored. Rape recovery simply is not as exciting a narrative as murder and fisticuffs as resolution. However, in the final season of *Poldark*, adapted not from Graham's novels but written directly for TV by Debbie Horsfield, we can see the influence of fourth-wave feminism and the impact of #MeToo on the show, which surprisingly does not disregard Morwenna's trauma. Horsfield, who faced criticism for her rewriting of the Ross-Elizabeth rape, boldly fills in the gaps between Graham's novels, and Morwenna's suffering takes center stage even in the midst of her happy second marriage. As she continues to flinch at Drake's touch, modern viewers are sure to recognize the symptoms of PTSD she exhibits. In an earlier episode she warned Drake before their marriage that she "cannot look on love—on carnal love—without revulsion. If your hands touched me, I would think of his hands, and if you kissed me, I'd think of his mouth, and the thought of flesh, any flesh against my own" (episode 4:7).

This potential for social critique in the show is, however, ultimately limited by its romance plot. Drake, of course, is constructed as a very modern hero, using the language of consent that twenty-first-century viewers are versed in when he promises Morwenna that he will "never ask you for more" (episode 4:8). And so, it is not surprising that the boyish good looks of the actor Harry Richardson who plays Drake attracted even more media and fan attention, and tabloids jokingly warned actor Aidan Turner that his Ross Poldark had a rival in the "battle of the heartthrobs" (Oliver 2018); meanwhile, comments on social media overwhelmingly praised Drake's "patience" with his bride and fans' anticipation for them to finally consummate their marriage is at last rewarded. After several episodes in season 5, in which the two are shown doing exactly what Drake had promised at the end of season 4, "just being together" side by side, without touching, Drake and Morwenna consummate their marriage and the birth of their child brings their story to a completion.

This recovery did trouble some fans, however: the series suggests that Morwenna's trauma is eventually cured through "the power of love" (Denby 2019). Men may be the cause of her suffering, but they are also, of course, the answer to it. Even Drake's (very likely ahistorical) sympathetic understanding undermines some of the political points the show could make about the way that patriarchy as a whole has been allowed to abuse women. The same law that allowed Ossie to exercise his "rights" will still apply to Drake as Morwenna's second husband, after all, but of course, he, as the romantic lead, would never exploit this power. We might recall here Taylor's suggestion, with which we opened this chapter, that judging the shortcomings of the past can imply that its problems are solved. We can see how, as she moves on to a fresh brighter future with a younger, more handsome husband, Morwenna's story reassures viewers that such atrocities as she endured are also left behind—even though, sadly, for many women they are not.

CONCLUSION

The quote in the title of this chapter is attributed to California state senator Bob Wilson in 1979, but can be said to sum up legal, social, and political attitudes toward marital rape even today. A decade after Wilson made that claim (in a speech to women lobbyists), across the ocean, the Court of Appeal in England continued to argue that it was "clear, well-settled and ancient law that a man cannot, as actor, be guilty of rape upon his wife, [a principle] which traces its history back to Hale's Pleas of the Crown" (Williamson 2017). Such arguments have not been made solely by men. Anti-feminist crusader, Phyllis Schlafly, for example, stated as late as 2007 that "by getting married, the woman has consented to sex, and I don't think you can call it rape" (quoted in Richardson 2020). The 2020 period drama, *Mrs. America*, likely mindful of Schlafly's public stance on the issue, imagined a scene in which a tired Schlafly (Cate Blanchett), recently returned from a trip, tries to put off her husband's sexual advances, until she resignedly lays back on the bed and looks away as he penetrates her. Equally disturbing was a reviewer's comment the next day in *Radio Times* that this scene only "borders on marital rape" (Carr 2020). Marital rape then differs from the other rapes we examine elsewhere in this book, in that for many people, and for a long time (perhaps even today), it was not really considered to be rape at all. Nevertheless, in between the first and second adaptations of *The Forsyte Saga* and *Poldark*, the awareness and attitudes about marital rape shifted significantly both in the United States and the United Kingdom, the two main markets for these programs, due in large part to books like Brownmiller's *Against Our Will* (1975) and Diana Russell's survey *Rape in Marriage* (1982), as well as the activism of "on the ground feminists" like WAR (Women Against Rape) who drew media attention to the issue with accounts of actual victims of marital rape (Williamson, 2017: 401). And the efforts of the media did make a difference. For example, in 1989, the *World in Action* TV program featured a special episode, "The Right to Rape," in which it presented an academic survey showing that 14 percent of married women in England alone had been raped and that 96 percent of women wished to see the law changed (Williamson 2017: 399). As Williamson notes, women's magazines also featured traumatic stories from victims, while even some British tabloids asserted that "no decent man could possibly think that rape inside marriage was any less evil than rape outside it." Even *The Daily Mail*, a conservative newspaper, agreed that "the law must shield wives from rape" (Williamson, 2017: 399).

And at last judges caught up in 1991 when the marital rape exemption was invalidated in the United Kingdom and in every state in the United States by 1993. Period dramas that address marital rape, like those discussed in this chapter, therefore do more than underscore the potentially oppressive nature of marriage in the past for women: they have been and are still viewed by predominantly female audiences within a context of increasing debate about the law in their own lifetime. Further, these stories still matter and are relevant to twenty-first-century adaptations because marital rape persists—as do legal and political defenses of it. For example, Counsel to Donald Trump, upon accusations that the leading Republican candidate for the 2016 Presidency had raped his first wife, expressed emphatically that "you cannot rape your spouse. And there's very clear case law" (Mandle 2015).

The rapes we examine in this chapter are different from others in this book because this is a crime which audiences would like to believe has been consigned to the past. Other plotlines put rape "back into history": these rapes make us, as viewers, glad that it *is* history. Apart from the first adaptations of *The Forsyte Saga* and *Poldark*, all the period dramas discussed here were made after rape within marriage was made illegal in the United Kingdom and the United States, and they hence remind the viewer to be grateful for our "more enlightened present" and the progress made for women over this time (Taylor 2016: 336). As always with the gains of feminism, however, this progress is limited and accompanied by pitfalls. Fan responses and misdirected sympathies in these shows reveal that misogyny is still alive and well (and internalized by many women), and that marital rape can be still represented as a joke, a punishment, or a minor obstacle in the way of romance. Bourke has suggested that "if we want to eradicate rape from the marital bedroom, legal reform is not enough," and we can see that very plainly on our television screens (2007: 328). Nonetheless, period dramas, which have so often been accused of romanticizing and glamorizing the past, in this regard at least draw attention to its shortcomings and its darkness. These dramas, more than any other aspect of our media, bear testament to the horrors that so many wives have endured throughout history.

NOTES

1. In recent years, Estrich has faced criticism for her legal defense of Fox News CEO Roger Ailes who was accused of sexual harassment by employee, Gretchen Carlson, in 2016. See Farhi (2016), https://www.washingtonpost.com/lifestyle

/style/feminist-hero-susan-estrich-fought-sexual-harassment-but-now-represents-roger-ailes-is-she-selling-out-or-standing-up/2016/08/04/904c22ce-5810-11e6-9aee-8075993d73a2_story.html.

2. According to *The Week* (Dec 2018), "A review of laws in 82 countries by women's rights organization Equality Now between 2014 and 2015 found ten countries currently allow spousal rape. Many more countries have legislation that does not cover marital rape and considers sex within marriage consensual by definition, and thus they do not punish it as a criminal offence."

3. Graham once boasted that a literary critic dubbed him an "instinctive feminist" and in his memoirs he explained how his books addressed "the rough deal women have." See Julie Anne Taddeo (2014) for a discussion of Graham's feminism.

Chapter 7

Rape and the Older Woman

Rape on our screens, with a few exceptions, tends to involve beautiful young women. Traditionally, rape scenes were gratuitous and designed to draw attention to an attractive actress's body as it is assaulted, as shown by the legendary poster for rape-revenge film *I Spit on Your Grave* (1978), which features the eroticized rear view of a scantily clad Demi Moore, an image that became famous all around the world (Campochiaro 2020). Period drama is no different: in the 1967 *The Forsyte Saga*'s marital rape scene, Irene's breasts almost pour out of her corset. Similarly, Black Jack Randall's attempted rape of Jamie's sister Jenny in *Outlander*'s first season involves his ripping of her bodice, exposing her bare breasts to the viewer and her brother: arguably this is not intended as an erotically charged moment, but because Jenny is a beautiful young woman the appeal to the male gaze is the same.

It is true that, statistically, young women are more likely to be the victims of rape: according to RAINN (the Rape, Abuse & Incest National Network), "Ages 12–34 are the highest risk years for rape and sexual assault . . . females ages 16–19 are four times more likely than the general population" to be assaulted (2020). But as Lazar notes, sexual violence against older women (sixty and over), while prevalent in the home and in care facilities, remains underreported (Lazar 2020) unless it involves what most legal authorities still deem a "real rape" (perpetrated by a stranger). Regardless of the victim's age, as Benn, Coote, and Gill note, "It is the very condition of being female that is unsafe . . . the Rape Counselling and Research Project declared 'women of all ages classes and lifestyles have been raped'" (1986). Of course, rape is a crime about power and violence, and it is not confined to those who are young and desirable. But this myth about victims persists in the public's mind between rape and young attractive women, as highlighted during Donald Trump's first run for president in 2016. When women came forward alleging he had sexually assaulted them years before, Trump's response to a cheering crowd of supporters was "Look at her. . . . You tell me what you think. I don't think so. I don't think so," which boiled down to a "she's too ugly to rape" defense. In response to E. Jean Carroll, who has accused Trump of raping her in a New York City department store dressing room in 1995, Trump noted of the now much older Carroll, "She's not my type" (Dastagir 2019). This "too ugly to rape" defense has been used by other prominent men in recent years. When French economist and politician Dominique Strauss-Kahn was accused of sexually assaulting a hotel maid in 2011, online commenters questioned whether he would have raped her given "her ugliness," while in March 2019, Italy's Justice Ministry ordered an inquiry into a court ruling that overturned a rape verdict in part because of an assertion the woman was "too ugly to be a rape victim" (Dastagir 2019).

If such a defense exists in the courts and in the White House, it is no surprise that popular culture also continues to promote a stereotype of young, pretty victims—such as *Game of Thrones*' (2015) Sansa Stark's rape on her wedding night as Theon was forced to watch—a scene not in the books and criticized by fans for its gratuitousness (Tovey 2015). As a result, most of the rapes we discuss in this book feature this kind of victim, with the few exceptions that are explored in this chapter. There is nothing positive for young women about being the demographic most often raped on screen, but such a focus says a great deal about the way we as a society view both rape and older women. Associating sexual violence with youth and beauty in this way suggests that rape is always, at some level, erotic; that there is a belief that viewers want to see attractive, nubile bodies being violated. It also indicates the invisibility of older women, that, to put it crudely, they are not even "worth" raping. Imelda Whelehan has explored cinema's treatment of women over forty in terms which are important to recall here:

> Producers and consumers of popular culture have reached a bizarrely schizophrenic impasse in which older women rarely pass scrutiny because there are no positive meanings that reconcile post-menopausal women to the body; the numerical fact of their age generally renders them not fit to be seen. Ageing stars are implicitly exhorted to leave their "sexiness" at the door of menopause or face ageist slurs. The culture of youthfulness pervades Western media and has done so since at least the early twentieth century. (Whelehan, 2013: 79)

Whelehan draws attention to a problem widely acknowledged, but mostly unresolved, in Hollywood and also on television: the BBC has, for example, been accused several times over the last few years of discriminating against older women, with several examples of prime-time female presenters being fired and replaced by younger ones (Holmwood 2009). If older women "are not fit to be seen" in unthreatening presenter roles, how much more controversial would they be in shows which directly refer to or make capital of their sexuality? Of course, this is also a problem in the United States:

> Media in the United States reflect a sexist and aging culture. The media operate from a white, adult, male world-view: thus older women are doubly marginalized and nearly invisible . . . beauty is a resource perceived to belong to young women; older women's bodies are perceived to be ugly, asexual and undesirable. (McHugh and Interligi, 2014: 92)

It is unsurprising, then, that images of sexually active women are rare on our big or small screens: examples like Nicole Kidman, who was forty-nine when she first appeared in *Big Little Lies* (2017–2019), tend to be produced by the stars themselves in response to the lack of good roles created by others. The huge success of this drama, and similar female-created ones like *The Morning Show* (2019–) (produced by and starring Jennifer Aniston), shows there is an appetite for seeing middle-aged women as glamorous, fully rounded, sexually active characters—but only if they are already huge Hollywood stars and look many years younger than they are.

If it is rare to see older women represented as sexual creatures (especially if they look their age), it is unsurprising that they cannot be victims of sexual violence. This is damaging for two reasons: one is that, like male rape, the fact this is underrepresented on screen silences the voices of the many older women who have, in real life, survived rape. Secondarily, it perpetuates, even at a fundamental level, this idea that rape is erotic. Many period dramas, especially those made post-#MeToo, seem to be trying dutifully to separate sex and violence on screen, but once a rape is shown, it seems almost impossible for it not to feel pornographic. A typical example is the rape of Lila in *My Beautiful Friend*, which we discuss briefly in our chapter on marital rape but will revisit here. That is certainly an "unambiguous" rape, meant to be sympathetic to the victim: it is upsetting to watch Lila (Gaia Girace) scream "No—I don't want you" repeatedly and be subdued when she is violently slapped across the face by her husband. However, when he then rips her nightdress open, the camera follows his gaze, focusing on her beautiful, youthful, naked body as he removes her underwear. Even though the camera returns to her frozen, agonized face a moment later, it feels like the damage has been done: if only momentarily, this was a titillating rape. A similar split consciousness occurs when George in *A Place to Call Home* imagines Sarah's rape—which we and he know to be a war crime in reality—as an erotic encounter, with Sarah's thirty-something beauty emphasized (as we discuss in chapter 4). In this drama we see more of George's tormenting fantasy than we do of the actual attacks Sarah endures in the concentration camp, and again the camera seems unable to resist the erotic power of rape, even while the script and plot itself requires the viewer to be horrified by it.

MIDDLE-AGED WOMEN AND RAPE ON TELEVISION: *APPLE TREE YARD* AND *MAD MEN*

If the rape of younger women on screen is so often eroticized, it is perhaps only with plots that deal with assault on older women that this pitfall can be avoided and the true horror of rape brought home. Of course, such a distinction is insulting in itself, but such plotlines do important work in reminding the viewer that this crime does not only happen to young women. It is still relatively unusual for a drama to feature such a story line, however. One of the first to do so was *The Sopranos* (1999–2007), and despite the statistical unlikeliness of its rape plot—stranger rape in a parking garage—Dr. Melfi's attack was groundbreaking in that it involved the kind of character we least expect to see raped on TV: a professional, older woman (*The Sopranos* further deviated from rape tropes in that Melfi [Lorraine Bracco] chooses not to tell her patient, mob boss Tony Soprano [James Gandolfini], who she knows would seek revenge on her behalf, and hence opts out of the usual rape-revenge plot, which so often makes rape a commentary on hegemonic masculinity). While Melfi, a middle-aged psychiatrist, seems like an unlikely victim, we know from real-life statistics that there is no age limit to this crime: as sexual violence scholar Sarah Cook points out, "We see that babies to women in their 90s are raped" (Cook quoted in Dastagir 2019).

The Sopranos finished in 2007, but in more recent years, some British television dramas have continued to explore middle-aged victim story lines. While *Apple Tree Yard* (2017), like *The Sopranos*, is not a period drama, the rape scene garnered intense media attention, and hence is worth discussion here. *Apple Tree Yard*, the BBC's four-part drama based on the novel by Louise Doughty, has been described as "the first honest portrayal of rape on TV" (Aroesti, 2017). It stars Emily Watson as Yvonne Carmichael, a fifty-ish scientist who embarks on an affair with a mysterious stranger she meets in the Houses of Parliament. At the end of the first episode, Yvonne is raped, not by her lover, but by a middle-aged coworker, George, whose previous interactions with Yvonne seemed harmless. As other TV critics have pointed out, the rape seems to come out of nowhere and yet, partly as a result of this felt more realistic than most rape portrayals (Aroesti, 2017). Most of the episode focuses on Yvonne, in a sexless marriage, discovering a new side of herself with her handsome lover, which leads her to dress differently and become more confident. It is this newfound sense that she is no longer invisible and sexless, in the way Whelehan suggests fifty-something women are expected to be, which seems to trigger her coworker George. After drinking too much at their office party, Yvonne accepts George's offer of a shared cab ride home; while she is waiting sleepily on his office sofa, he says angrily, "I smell sex on you," and he strikes her twice before pinning her down on the sofa and raping her. In this way the rape is framed as a punishment for enjoying one's sexuality as an older woman.

This scene is oddly reminiscent of the rape of Joan Holloway (Christina Hendricks) by her fiancé in season 2 of *Mad Men* (2007–2025)—a woman we would not ordinarily describe as "middle-aged" but who in the glamorous world of 1960s advertising is reminded that she is no longer young. In an earlier episode, a male coworker maliciously pinned her driver's license to the bulletin board, revealing that Joan, despite the shapely figure which she is so proud of, is in her thirties; her much younger subordinate at the time, Peggy Olson (Elisabeth Moss), says with a hint of glee, "I never would have guessed you were in your thirties" (episode 2:2). In a later episode (2:12), when Joan shows her fiancé her place of work, it becomes increasingly evident that Greg (Samuel Page) resents her success and the ease with which she talks to her male bosses (Greg senses that Roger and Joan have a sexual history). When he asks to see her boss (Don Draper)'s office, Greg says in a commanding tone, "Pretend like I'm your boss." She hesitates, pours him a drink, but when he comes up behind her, she tells him, "Not in here," but he ignores her pleas of "No" and "Stop" as he lowers her to the floor, pins her arms down, and then presses his hand over her face—she looks away as he finishes. Aired in 2009, almost a decade before #MeToo, this scene was debated on social media by fans who were not in agreement if this was "really rape," suggesting that Joan, as a 1960s woman, would not understand what happened to her in such terms. This fan reaction might not surprise us, given many others like it we quote in this book, but Christina Hendricks, the actress who played Joan, was horrified:

> The rape was a shocker-but the audience reactions were perhaps more disturbing. What's astounding is when people say things like, "Well, you know that episode where Joan sort of got raped?" Or they say rape and use quotation marks with their fingers, . . . I'm like, "What is that you are doing? Joan got raped!" It illustrates how similar people are today, because we're still questioning whether it's a rape. It's almost like, "Why didn't you just say bad date?" (quoted in Peterson, 2009)

As discussed in chapter 6, this further emphasizes the reluctance of even twenty-first-century viewers to consider marital rape (being engaged as the equivalent of marriage in Joan's case) in the same way as other sex crimes. But it is also an attack bent on diminishing female power in the workplace: Joan is good at her job; Greg resents her for it, and rape is the easiest way to punish her.[1]

Like Joan, Yvonne in *Apple Tree Yard* is also raped in the office, likely in part in an attempt to undermine her achievements in that area. George has already been overshadowed by her success when she is invited to testify before a Parliamentary committee about her research. By reducing her to an unwilling sex object, George may hope she will cease to be a threat in the public sphere (and after the rape he sends her threatening messages which succeed in making her quit her job). We do not see the rape itself—just fragments in flashback, with the camera focused on Yvonne's face—but its brutality is made clear later when we learn from Yvonne that it lasted for hours, and that he treated her "as a collection of holes" before he forced her to drive home in the shared Uber cab. Its trauma continues into the next episode when Yvonne tells her lover Mark (Ben Chaplin) that she has internal bruising and an anal tear. In an interview for *The Irish News*, Steven Elder, who plays George, explained why the scene was necessary:

> I also knew from the onset that it would be filmed very much in a non-titillating way and that it would be about what it is about, which is about ugliness and about violence and in this case violence perpetrated by a psychologically weak man.

Citing the statistic from Rape Crisis UK that 90 percent of those raped or attacked know their assailant, Elder added, "I do feel a responsibility to use it as a forum to discuss this issue" (qtd in *The Irish News*, 2017). The show also draws attention to the difficulties of reporting rape, due to a continuing culture of victim-blaming and judging. Yvonne even drives to a police station, but then decides she cannot report what has happened, partly because of the impact on her family, and partly because the fact that she had a lover and had been with him earlier that night before the rape harms her credibility. Yvonne is an anomaly, then: not only an older, comfortably middle-class scientist, but one who has been sexually active at the time of her rape. This might be why there were multiple complaints to the BBC about the graphic nature of the attack, which seems surprising given the act itself is not shown. Like *Outlander*'s season 5 finale rape of Claire (which we discuss below), there was a pre-air warning and a hotline number for sexual assault victims. Perhaps audiences are more accustomed to rapes which are presented as "gentler" and more eroticized, rather than drawing attention to physical damage and brutality.

PUTTING THE MIDDLE-AGED WOMAN IN HER PLACE IN *OUTLANDER* AND *PEAKY BLINDERS*

Period drama has traditionally been supportive of, and heavily populated with, older actresses: what would *Downton Abbey* be without the relationship between the Dowager Countess (Maggie Smith) and Isobel Crawley (Penelope Wilton)? And Judy Dench has stolen the show in almost every historical fiction she appears in, from the almost entirely female *Cranford* (2007) to her turns as Queen Victoria (*Mrs. Brown*, 1997) and Elizabeth I (*Shakespeare in Love*, 1998). Indeed, as Niall Richardson has noted,

> The Heritage Film . . . has not only been considerably more sympathetic to the representation of the older woman but can be seen to draw a deliberate conflation between the heritage of Britain (especially its grand architecture) and the older bodies as exemplars of everything that is "great" about British culture—past and present. (2019: 28)

Certainly, most of the older actors who appear in period dramas have become national treasures in Britain, and as such are immune to rape plotlines. Slightly younger and/or still sexually active women, however, clearly occupy a much more liminal and problematic space. Claire Fraser (Caitriona Balfe) in *Outlander* and Polly Gray (Helen McCrory) in *Peaky Blinders* are both middle-aged, menopausal women who experience brutal rape both connected, in different ways, to their experiences as working women and to attempts to take away the power they have worked for.

As we have already discussed, rape has been a constant part of Claire's life. From the moment she passed through the stones from the post–World War II era into eighteenth-century Scotland, she suffers repeated attempted and actual acts of sexual violence, but in middle age, after establishing a career as a surgeon and reuniting with Jamie (Sam Heughan), it seems that rape may finally elude her. As discussed in chapter 2, in season 4, it is her twenty-two-year-old daughter Brianna who is raped by the pirate Bonnet: when he previously encounters Claire, his only interest in her is to rob her of her wedding ring, suggesting she is now safe from sexual assault. This makes the gang rape of Claire in season 5, filmed post-#MeToo, all the more shocking—but also an important reminder that rape is not a crime of passion but of power. Sexual violence is used by her assailants to punish Claire for her work empowering the local women and giving them the knowledge and means to control their own body and its reproductive capacity.

There are some striking differences from the 2005 source text: Claire's rape occurs in book 6, *A Breath of Snow and Ashes*, in Gabaldon's series, and is committed by a nameless, faceless man. Gabaldon even explained in a *New York Times* interview (Vineyard 2020) that "Claire is only penetrated by one man in the book, *who is not violent about it*" (emphasis added)—a statement that is troubling in itself. In season 5 of the TV series, however, she is gang-raped by Lionel Brown (Ned Dennehy) and several of his men, who kidnap, bind, and gag her, before deciding to rape her after more than a day in captivity (See figure 7.1). In ripping her clothes with a knife, one of her attackers slices at her chest, barely missing her breast (which is not exposed to the viewer's eye), and she is beaten about the face. Later, when we see her at home, unclothed, her entire body is bruised.

Just what is the purpose of this rape, or to quote Claire from season 1, episode 2, "Is there ever a good reason for rape?" It is clearly an act of punishment by Brown, an abusive husband (and perpetrator of marital rape), angry over his discovery in the previous episode that Claire is the doctor whose contraceptive advice has been followed by his own wife to avoid getting pregnant. Brown seeks revenge on the woman he blames for his wife's sexual education and resistance. During the assault, which is spread out over two days, Brown taunts her with

> Aren't you the clever one, Dr. Rawlings? . . . you're gonna repent for your sin . . . spreading dangerous ideas, what you mean? Telling women how to deceive their husbands, how to deny them their God-given rights, telling my wife to avoid my bed.

When she warns that if they touch her they will all be dead by dawn, one of the group's men reminds them that she has a reputation as a "conjure woman" but Brown, refusing to show weakness before his men, gags Claire, telling her

Figure 7.1   Claire Taken Hostage by Brown's Gang in *Outlander,* Episode 5:12 (2020).
Source: Screen grab by Julie Anne Taddeo.

"not one more damn word"—then proceeds to beat and rape her: "I'm gonna put some manners on you." Previously feared as a witch or "conjure woman," Claire is now no longer the commanding figure who Brown and his men need to fear or respect. Taken away from her surgery and prosperous home, dragged through the mud, her clothes torn, her hair loose, she has the status for which she has worked hard over the years taken away. Sexual violence is useful to her attackers as a weapon to undermine power and authority and put Claire in her place, as it has countless women before her, and as we also see it do to another successful woman in *Apple Tree Yard*. Indeed, this plot is a dramatization of Susan Brownmiller's famous declaration in *Against Our Will* that rape is "nothing more or less than a conscious process of intimidation by which all men keep all women in a state of fear" (1975: 10).

After the rape, Brown gloats, "Not so high and mighty now, are we?" and invites the others "for a go with the hedge whore." As such, he is making a statement that this is not an act of desire (the "hedge whore" makes that clear) but punishment of a woman who refused to "be afraid." One of the men who doesn't take part in the gang rape, a Native American named Donner, reveals to Claire that he is a time traveler, and that he recognized her as one too because "you don't act afraid of men. Most of the women from now do," in a reminder of the progression of feminism for women through history. Rather than help her, however, he restores the gag to her mouth and warns, almost with glee, "You ought to act more afraid": once again, misogyny has changed little over the centuries. Later, upon her rescue, learning of the men now killed by her husband's own gang in retaliation, she asks if there was an "Indian among them"—and though she says he didn't hurt her, "he didn't help me": once again, *Outlander* takes pains to remind us how complicit the bystander is in acts of rape.

Claire is not only being punished for being educated and successful, of course. Also implicit in the series is that she, like Yvonne, is problematic for being menopausal and yet still desirable and sexually active: for not leaving her "'sexiness' at the door of menopause" as Whelehan puts it (Whelehan, 2013: 79). We have already been made aware of Claire's age in the previous episode when she awakens in the middle of the night, her night dress soaked in sweat, seeking fresh air by the window. Curiously, though a doctor and dispenser of sexual education to other women, it doesn't resonate with her that she is having a hot flash. It has been easy to forget that Claire is meant to be around fifty years old, for a few gray streaks and crinkles around the eyes do little to detract from the beauty of actress Catriona Balfe, who is only in her early forties in real life. Again, if middle-aged women are allowed sexuality on screen, they cannot actually look middle-aged (Jamie's age is only referenced when he uses eyeglasses to read, and both their bodies are as toned and youthful looking as ever). It is significant, however, that this menopausal moment is followed by Jamie licking the salt off her skin and then performing cunnilingus on her, making clear that he still very much desires her (supposedly though not visibly) aging body. That Claire is still very much a sexually active and desirous woman is made evident when Jamie apologizes for earlier falling asleep on her, "You wanted me and I fell asleep without touching you"—and now awake, he jokes, "You could have raised me from the dead for this." But that their sex is no longer at risk of being procreative is hinted at the next day as she clinically studies his sperm under her microscope: when Jamie asks whose "seed" they are, she replies, "Yours of course, I woke up in custody of them this morning."

That this intimate, consensual act will be followed later that week by such sexual violence is reminiscent of Brianna's rape plotline, in which she has loving consensual sex with Roger to make clear the difference between that and her rape by Bonnet the same night. And, like Brianna's rape, *Outlander* shows that it is conscious of its post-#MeToo responsibilities, in that Claire's rape is filmed to focus on her face rather than the penetration of her body (which remains clothed) and moves back and forth between Claire's present and her imagination, as she disassociates and takes herself to Thanksgiving in a bright sunny house in the 1960s. Instead of the exposed breasts we so often see when younger women are assaulted, the camera focuses on her wide open eyes, revealing her to be traumatized and disconnected from what is happening to her body, until she hears gunfire and screams, returning her to her present attack, as Jamie and his men have at last come to her rescue. And far from looking erotic, the normally immaculate Claire looks bedraggled as a captive, the gray streaks in her hair aging her and seeming suddenly more visible. She has aged years in these hours and her vulnerability is more pronounced than in any of her previous encounters with sexual predators over the years.

Season 5 of *Outlander*, then, is an interesting feminist development for the show: showing a woman who is still sexually active, desiring, and desirable while being menopausal is remarkable in itself. Furthermore, the rape plotline exposes male anxiety about women with power and displays that, rather than being about sex (the uncontrollable male sex drive we still hear so much about), rape is an attempt to punish and intimidate women. Claire's rape stresses the violence and suffering of the crime but shows her refusal to be oppressed or shattered by this, "I won't be. I won't," as she reminds Jamie that she has already suffered and survived the loss of two husbands and their first child, and a world war. Moreover, she refuses to be desexualized by what has happened: in the closing scene of the episode, Claire is naked in bed in Jamie's arms, and tells him she once again feels "safe." Still, this representation of "healing through sex," also hinted at by the post-rape sex between Yvonne and Mark in *Apple Tree Yard* (and another version perhaps of Morwenna "healed through love" that we discuss in chapter 6), is problematic for many real-life victims. Within the context of a TV series determined to show the audience a sexually active middle-aged woman, however, it is important that the rape survivor is not rendered "invisible" sexually by the crime.

As the season finale aired in 2020, the rape's long-term traumatic impact on Claire is yet to be seen, but finally it is worth noting that this rape, like so many others in *Outlander*, immediately sacrifices some of its feminist credentials by becoming part of the post-rape male vengeance scenario we discuss earlier. It is Jamie and his men (including Roger, who was unable to protect his own wife from rape) who rescue Claire and rapidly kill her attackers. One of Jamie's men asks, holding out a knife to Claire, "Will you have your vengeance upon them, Mistress?," but Jamie reminds them of her oath to uphold, not take, life. "It is myself that kills for her," he asserts—and Fergus and Ian chime in, "And I." Claire is not empowered enough to take revenge herself, and the repercussions from this violent revenge will dominate the next series, as a long final voice-over from Jamie (it's usually Claire's words that open and close an episode) suggests. Claire's rape, like so many others on TV, likely won't be about her long-term recovery but about two male heads of their clans, waging war. The only twist here is that the actual killer of Brown is a woman: stepdaughter Marsali (Lauren Lyle) does for Claire what she couldn't do herself. Telling Jamie about Brown's murder, Marsali explains, "He thought me no better than the dirt under his boot. A mere woman of no consequence," and the show is at least determined to have such misogyny suitably punished.

AUNT POLLY'S RAPE IN *PEAKY BLINDERS*

Given the violent nature of *Peaky Blinders*, a series about an interwar Birmingham gangster family, rape should not feel so out of context. Nevertheless, the season 3 rape of the Shelby matriarch, "Aunt Polly" Gray, was indeed shocking—as Polly's "toughness" (she swaggers down the city streets side by side with her gangster nephews, drinks and smokes heavily, and curses just like the men) seemed to make her immune to any kind of assault. Though the actress playing her, Helen McCrory, was closer to fifty at the time, Polly is in her mid-forties yet "still breaking hearts" as Tommy Shelby comments. Indeed, McCrory became during the past decade of her career a popular figurehead for the desirable and desiring middle-aged woman. Several of her roles were forty-something women in love with younger men—women, who, as she pointed out, "no longer feel it inappropriate to be sexual at forty in the way many did 50 or 60 years ago" (Kellaway 2013). Polly, too, is sexually liberated and engages in many acts of consensual sex throughout the series. Yet the one man whose attentions she previously has rebuffed, Tommy's nemesis Inspector Campbell (played by Sam Neill), has been biding his time.

In her youth Polly had a child out of wedlock, Michael (Finn Cole), with whom she has been reunited in season 2, but despite her good intentions to keep him honest, Michael gets swept up in the Shelby family business. When he is arrested by Campbell for arson, the latter knows his chance to exercise his power over Polly has at last arrived. She visits Campbell in his office at the jail and bluntly proposes an exchange of favors: sex for the release of her son Michael from prison. Instead of accepting Polly's offer, however, Campbell proceeds to brutally rape her on his desk: "I need you to cry," he tells Polly whose repeated defiance angers him (see figure 7.2). As he bends her back over the desk and unbuttons her dress, he spits out, "You think you're so respectable . . . I know what you are, you gypsy slut." When she talks back, he strikes her face and again demands that she cry; the scene fades as he forces her back onto the desk, and we next see Polly bathing in her tin tub, drunk and looking older, wincing in pain. When she waits outside the prison gate the next day for Michael's release, her son looks at her with contempt rather than gratitude and reveals the police told him *what she did*, "They thought it was funny. Maybe it is," he says.

Polly tells no one that Campbell raped her. Her niece attributes her moodiness to drinking too much, and as the head of the family, Polly is reluctant to reveal any vulnerabilities. When Tommy plots to kill Campbell in season 2, episode 6, she insists that it be her that "finishes" the Inspector, but Tommy doesn't ask why. Armed with a gun, she confronts Campbell in a phone booth at the racetrack, but he thinks he can convince her to not shoot, even telling her that she has romantic feelings for him. In response, she says, "Small and weak, that's how you like it. Well, this time small and weak has got a gun." As he dies at her feet, Polly utters the usual tagline that we hear after so many of the series' murders committed by her nephews: "Don't fuck with the Peaky Blinders" and the rock band, Black Rebel Motorcycle Club, plays as she struts out of the booth, into the crowd, with blood on her dress.

While viewers cheered Polly's revenge—and as we discussed in chapter 2, it is rare to see a woman avenge herself in period drama—any attempt at sensitively treating her rape and its traumatic aftermath gives way to making this yet another "hip" moment in this series that treats all forms of violence so casually. As befitted such a talented actor, though, McCrory has a devoted fan base who responded positively to this plotline. Airing in 2018, post-#MeToo, Polly's rape also resonated with many viewers:

> But I can't tell you how often I've received letters, or people come up to me in the street, and women tell me these extraordinary stories, and what they felt

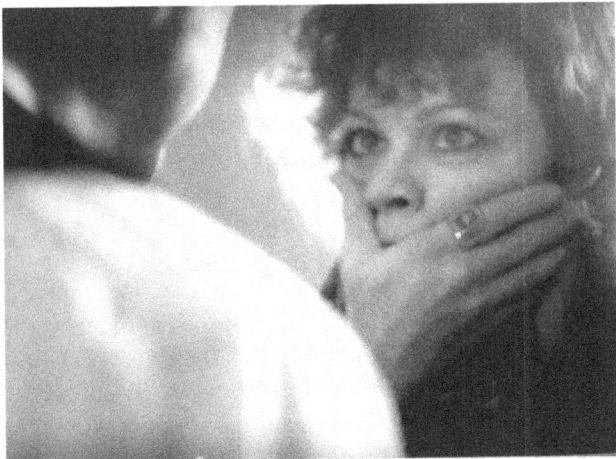

Figure 7.2 Campbell Strikes Polly Before Raping Her in His Office in *Peaky Blinders*, Episode 2:5 (2014). *Source*: Screen grab by Julie Anne Taddeo.

when they saw Polly talk about it. . . . And I'm so aware that when you play these parts and play those moments, there is a triangle of ghosts behind you, of people that have never told their stories. (McCrory quoted in Rodger 2019)

McCrory's interview did not raise the issue of Polly's age, or if some of the victims of sexual assault who contacted her were middle-aged or older women. Perhaps the significance of this omission is that survivors themselves do not recognize such differences as relevant: rape is a violation no matter the age of those attacked. And, by showing the rape of a tough and resourceful matriarch like Polly, this series reinforces the message that anyone can be a victim.

CONCLUSION

Most rapes of middle-aged and older women in real life occur in their private homes. As Lazar notes in regard to Canadian and American case law, such acts are "an attack on the privacy, autonomy, and confidence of victims" (2020:245). The other place at which women should, though often do not, feel secure and confident is at their place of work, and that is the setting for most of the period drama rapes we discuss here. Recent studies in the United Kingdom and the United States suggest that over 50 percent of women face sexual harassment and/or assault in the workplace at some point in their careers.[2] Joan and Yvonne, as discussed earlier, are assaulted at work; Claire's home is also her place of work when it is invaded by Brown and his gang; Inspector Campbell uses his office, the place where he exercises the most power, as the site of Polly's rape. It is of course not accidental that these workspaces are where middle-aged women are attacked on screen. Naomi Woolf wrote in her influential book, *The Beauty Myth*, how the cosmetic surgery and antiaging industries target and attempt to demoralize women "in the decades from forty to sixty . . . when most are at the peak of their powers" (1991: 230). Sexual violence works in the same way as this kind of industrialized violence, taking away security and confidence at an age when many women have worked hard for decades to achieve both. Hence the—often especially violent and upsetting—rapes of older women on screen serve a valuable function. They remind us that the crime is about power, male insecurity, and misogyny, not desire: something easily forgotten if we focus only on the many eroticized rapes of beautiful younger women on screen.

We have asked elsewhere in this book if "TV is raping women too much" and in one way, showing yet more violence against women on screen is scarcely a cause for jubilation. But the dramas here also celebrate middle-aged female sexuality before and after the attack and take pains to show it ultimately undefeated by rape. This is in itself still rare: popular culture, on the whole, when it considers this age group (women in their forties to sixties, or even older) ultimately treats women's sexuality with comedy (e.g., *Calendar Girls* [2004], *Book Club* [2018], and *Grace and Frankie* [2015–]) or horror, (most famously, *Sunset Boulevard* [1950], *Whatever Happened to Baby Jane* [1962], and more recently, *Greta* [2019] in what has since come to be called "hagsploitation" films). And, of course, older men, on average, appear nearly ten times more frequently than older women in the media (Loughrey 2019). Period drama, with its female-centric plots, addresses these gaps. But its middle-aged rape survivors still tend to have retained some of their former youthfulness and beauty: victims who are older still are left out. This chapter does not include those Lazar refers to as "the missing victims"—women over the age of sixty whose rapes often constitute "elder abuse" (2020:246), as we have not found any period dramas which include such crimes. Age, it seems, is still an important factor in how, or if, television portrays rape.

NOTES

1. There was a similar reluctance by *Game of Thrones*' showrunners and some fans to name what Jaime Lannister (Nikolaj Coster-Waldau) does to Cersei Lannister in 2014's season 4, episode 3 as "rape": perhaps because she's villainous and older (played at the time by forty-year-old actress Lena Headey)—and previously engaged in consensual sex with her brother—Cersei elicits less sympathy from viewers. Despite her repeated pleas of "no" and "don't," the act, according to the episode's

director, Alex Graves, "becomes consensual by the end" (quoted in Lyons 2014). Yet again, an older, powerful woman, who we already learned had been repeatedly raped by her first husband, is brutally subjugated, this time by her brother, who, when she tells him, "It isn't right," replies, "I don't care."

2. See https://www.safeline.org.uk/sexual-harassment-in-the-workplace-is-found-to-affect-over-half-of-uk-women/ for the UK and https://iwpr.org/iwpr-publications/briefing-paper/sexual-harassment-and-assault-at-work-understanding-the-costs/ for U.S. statistics.

Conclusion

As we send this book off to press, we are already frustrated by new rapes being aired on our small screens which we cannot cover. Television critics have been asking for years if "TV is raping women too much" (Valby 2014), and in one sense, of course they are. It does seem that sexual violence is too often used, lazily, as shorthand for backstory and drama: to liven up a plot, give depth to a character, or create a catalyst for conflict and revenge. In fact, so commonplace are rape plots that *Hannibal* (2013–2015) showrunner Bryan Fuller made headlines for *not* using rape in his hit U.S. show, explaining, "It's so overexploited, it becomes callous.... You're reduced to using shorthand, and I don't think there can be a shorthand for that violation" (quoted in Vanstone 2016). Plenty of shows do indeed feel "callous" in their often exploitative, often eroticized, frequent portrayal of rape.

As we have shown in this book, period drama, more than any other genre, relies heavily on rape as a plot device, to make their stories about past women's lives "feel authentic," and to add grittiness to their representation of the past. However, unlike two-hour films, and many detection-driven crime procedurals, period dramas have the luxury of multiple episodes, and often multiple seasons, to explore the larger consequences of rape. As a result, they do not need to resort to "shorthand" but can (if they so choose) unpack the survivor's trauma, the impact on those in their immediate community, and the long-term effects of the crime. As we have discussed here, many dramas do indeed do this with compassion and depth, and many viewers, some of whom are themselves survivors of rape, have been moved or helped by these stories. At a conference recently, we were asked if there is such a thing as a positive, helpful representation of sexual violence on television, and we hope we have shown here that many shows do feature rapes which feel necessary and which make important points about survivors or perpetrators, and which expose certain rape myths. Sometimes, of course, even the same programs fall into old traps of representation: focusing narrative attention on the husband or lover of the victim, and his revenge, is probably one of the most common. Representing violent rape by a stranger, instead of by someone much closer to home, as the norm is another. What these dramas all do, however, is show us women telling the truth. None of the period drama rapes we found feature a false accusation of rape, and implicit here is an acknowledgment that such a thing is rare. Often, the victims' stories are not accepted or acted upon by other characters, but almost always the viewer has witnessed them and can vouch for their authenticity. There is a powerful message here—from even the most conservative dramas—about the need to believe accusations, which our courts and police forces would do well to listen to.

It is possible to show the past without rape. The three-season Swedish series *The Restaurant* ([2017–] set between 1945 and 1971) illustrated that it is possible to tell compelling stories without resorting to sexual violence plots. But is it right to do so? What the #MeToo and #TimesUp movements, and many more like the Everyday Sexism Project, have shown over the last few years is that sexual violence is, and long has been, endemic in our society. The first step in dealing with this reality is to acknowledge the extent of the problem, and period dramas have helped us do that. Perhaps the sheer number of rapes they feature is only shocking because we do not like to think how many people have been victims throughout history. The more recent trend of male rapes, particularly in *Outlander*, should not be read as an "equal opportunity" victimization either, but an acknowledgment that men also are affected by this crime, and even more likely than women to stay silent about it.

Completing this book in the midst of a global pandemic has reminded us of the power of period drama. Television is a major driver in the public's interest in history and also one of the best means of escape and comfort in times of crisis. We saw this with the huge success of *Downton Abbey* as the world emerged out of the 2008 economic recession, but COVID-19 lockdowns and streaming services have meant even more time and opportunity to binge-watch over the last year. Television is the one pleasure we can safely and easily access, and the international appeal of shows like *Bridgerton* indicates how such times of crisis fuel nostalgia-induced viewing habits. As we have argued here, however, rape is the one area that these dramas do not encourage us to be nostalgic about. Instead, they often suggest we should be grateful for modernity, for the gains of several waves of feminism, and, in particular, for the changes in rape law in the twentieth century. But these dramas should not prompt a collective sigh of relief that such crimes and abuses no longer happen, for we know that they do. Indeed, viewed differently, these dramas perform important "antirape work" (Projansky 2001) by showing the viewer how little things have actually changed for women, and how much progress is still needed before the horrors we see on screen actually become a thing of the past.

Bibliography

Abdullah-Khan, Noreen. 2008. *Male Rape: The Emergence of a Social and Legal Issue*. London: Palgrave.

Alexenko, et al. (n.d.). "Victim or survivor?: Terminology from investigation through prosecution," https://sakitta.org/toolkit/docs/Victim-or-Survivor-Terminology-from-Investigation-Through-Prosecution.pdf (accessed 9 September 2021).

Andersson, Ulrika, et al. (eds.). 2019. *Rape Narratives in Motion*. Springer International Publishing AG. http://ebookcentral.proquest.com/lib/ulster/detail.action?docID=5739667 (accessed 10 April 2021).

A Place to Call Home (Seven Network, 2013–2018).

Apple Tree Yard (BBC, 2016).

Banished (BBC Two, 2015).

BBCNews 2016. "Poldark 'rape' scene sparks controversy," https://www.bbc.com/news/entertainment-arts-37749637 (Accessed 10 October 2018).

BBC News 2018. "Coronation street male rape scene: Helplines see spike in calls," https://www.bbc.co.uk/news/uk-england-manchester-43498590 (accessed 1 June 2021).

BBCNews 2019. "UK film age rating rules get stricter for scenes of sexual violence," https://www.bbc.com/news/entertainment-arts-46889982 (accessed 24 May 2021).

BBCTV blog http://www.bbc.co.uk/blogs/tv (Accessed 4 June 2018).

Beevor, Antony 2015. "By banning my book, Russia is deluding itself about its past," *The Guardian*, https://www.theguardian.com/commentisfree/2015/aug/05/banning-book-russia-past-holocaust-red-army-antony-beevor (accessed 29 May 2021).

Benn, Melissa, Coote, Anna, and Gill, Tess. 1986. *The Rape Controversy*. 3rd Rev. and Updated ed. London: NCCL Rights for Women Unit.

Bennice, Jennifer A. and Resick, Patricia A. 2003. "Marital Rape: History, Research, and Practice," *Trauma, Violence & Abuse*, vol. 4:3 (July 2003), pp. 228–246.

Berridge, Susan 2010. *Serialised sexual violence in teen television drama series*. University of Glasgow, PhD thesis. http://theses.gla.ac.uk/2326/ (accessed 13 October 2018).

Bignell, Jonathan 2003. *An Introduction to Television Studies*. Abingdon-on-Thames: Routledge.
Black Christmas (Directed by Sophia Takal, 2019).
Blake, Meredith. 2016. "'Outlander' Showrunner Ron Moore discusses "unflinching" rape scene and Season 2 reset," *LA Times*, http://www.latimes.com/entertainment/tv/showtracker/la-et-st-outlander-season-2-reset-ron-moore-jamie-rape-20160408-story.html (accessed 4 June 2018).
Bletchley Circle (ITV, 2012–2014).
Bonner, Mehera. 2015. "Outlander Finale Recap: Jamie Fraser Raped in Most Controversial Scene Yet," *US Weekly*, http://www.usmagazine.com/entertainment/news/outlander-finale-shocker-jamie-fraser-is-raped----read-the-recap-2015305 (Accessed 1 June 2021).
Bourke, Joanna. 2007. *Rape: Sex Violence History*. Berkley: Shoemaker Hoard.
Bridgerton (Netflix, 2020–).
Bridges, Ana J., Wosnitzer, Robert, Scharrer, Erica, Sun, Chyng, & Liberman, Rachael. 2010. "Aggression and Sexual Behavior in Best-Selling Pornography Videos: A Content Analysis Update," *Violence against Women,* vol. 16, pp. 1065–1085.
Brownmiller, Susan. 1975. *Against Our Will: Men, Women and Rape*. New York: Simon & Schuster.
Bucksbaum, Sydney. 2018. "How 'Outlander' Plans to Handle Season 4 Rape Storyline Amid the #MeToo Climate," *The Hollywood Reporter*, https://www.hollywoodreporter.com/live-feed/outlander-season-4-spoilers-rape-storyline-explained-1096775 (accessed 14 November 2018).
Byrne, Katherine. 2015. "New Developments in Heritage: The Recent Dark Side of Downton "Downer" Abbey," in *Upstairs and Downstairs: British Costume Drama Television from The Forsyte Saga to Downton Abbey*, edited by James Leggott and Julie Anne Taddeo, London: Rowman & Littlefield, pp. 177–189.
Byrne, Katherine. 2015. *Edwardians on Screen: From Downton Abbey to Parade's End*. London: Palgrave Macmillan.
Byrne, Katherine. 2018. "Pathological masculinities: Syphilis and the medical profession in The Frankenstein Chronicles," in *Conflicting Masculinities: Men in Television Period Drama,* edited by Byrne et al. I. B. Tauris, pp. 146–162.
Campochiaro, Michael. 2020. "The legend of Demi Moore's backside," https://aftermoviediner.com/feed/articles/the-legend-of-demi-moores-backside-or-i-strip-teased-on-your-grave (accessed 2 June 2021).
Cannon, Nick. 2019. "Poldark's Ellise Chappell: 'I cry when I think about what Morwenna has been through!'" https://www.whatsontv.co.uk/news/poldarks-ellise-chappell-cry-morwenna-588124/ (accessed 19 May 2021).
Capers, Bennett. 2011. "Real Rape Too," *California Law Review*, vol. 99:5, pp. 1259–1307.
Carr, Flora. 2020. "Mrs America review: Cate Blanchett humanises TV drama's pastel-clad anti-heroine Phyllis Schlafly," *Radio Times*, https://www.radiotimes.com/tv/drama/mrs-america-review-cate-blanchett/ (accessed 10 September 2021).

Chalmers, Beverley. 2015. *Birth, Sex and Abuse: Women's Voices Under Nazi Rule*. Guilford: Grosvenor House Publishing.

Chaney, Jen. 2018. "2018 is the summer of #MeToo TV," *Vulture*, 25 May, https://www.vulture.com/2018/05/2018-is-the-summer-of-metoo-tv.html (accessed 24 March 2019).

Chow, Karen. 1999. "Popular Sexual Knowledges and Women's Agency in 1920s England: Marie Stopes's *Married Love* and E.M. Hull's *The Sheik*," *Feminist Review*, vol. 63:1, pp. 64–87.

Cohen, Claire. 2014. *Male Rape is a Feminist Issue: Feminism, Governmentality and Male Rape*, https://link.springer.com/chapter/10.1057/9781137035103_1 (accessed 1 June 2021).

Cohn, Carol. 2013. "Women and Wars: Towards a Conceptual Framework," in *Women and Wars*, edited by Carol Cohn. Cambridge: Polity Press.

Coronation Street (ITV, 1960–).

Cosslett, Rhiannon Lucy and Bidisha. 2013. "Was the Downton abbey rape scene acceptable TV?" *The Guardian*, https://www.theguardian.com/commentisfree/2013/oct/08/downton-abbey-rape-scene-acceptable-tv (accessed 10 April 2021).

Coy, Maddy, ed. 2012. *Prostitution, Harm and Gender Inequality: Theory, Research and Policy*. Abingdon-on-Thames: Routledge.

Cuklanz, Lisa M. 1996. *Rape on Trial: How the Mass Media Construct Legal Reform and Social Change*. Philadelphia: University of Pennsylvania Press.

Cuklanz, Lisa M. 1999. *Rape on Prime Time: Television, Masculinity, and Sexual Violence*. Philadelphia: University of Pennsylvania Press.

Das Boot (Sky One, 2018–).

Dastagir, Alia E. 2019. "Experts explain why the 'too ugly to rape' argument doesn't hold up," *USA Today*, https://www.usatoday.com/story/news/nation/2019/06/25/trump-calls-accuser-e-jean-carroll-not-my-type-its-rape-myth-too-ugly/1554488001/ (accessed 4 June 2021).

Davies, Caroline. 2020. "Is she hiding in a submarine? In a bunker? The hunt for Ghislaine Maxwell," *The Guardian*, https://www.theguardian.com/lifeandstyle/2020/dec/15/is-she-hiding-in-a-submarine-in-a-b2unker-the-hunt-for-ghislaine-maxwell (accessed 5 May 2021).

Deacon, Michael. 2014. "'The Fall' may be 'repulsive' but it's right to show the graphic murder of women," *The Telegraph*, http://www.telegraph.co.uk/culture/tvandradio/11228749/the-fall-bbc-2-murder-women-gillian-anderson.html (accessed 6 June 2018).

Debnath, Neela. 2017. "Poldark season 3: Charity Rape Crisis breaks silence on 'harrowing' Morwenna scene," *Express*, https://www.express.co.uk/showbiz/tv-radio/836985/Poldark-season-3-Charity-Rape-Crisis-Morwenna-Whitworth-BBC (accessed 20 May 2021).

Debnath, Neela. 2015. "Outlander star Caitriona Balfe on filming rape scenes and sexual violence in the show," *Express*, http://www.express.co.uk/showbiz/tv-radio/580949/Outlander-Caitriona-Balfe-rape-scenes-sexual-violence (accessed 1 June 2021).

Denby, Odessa. 2019. "The Trouble with Morwenna," *blog post*, https://odessadenby.medium.com/the-trouble-with-morwenna-357d04d92b50 (accessed 5 May 2021).

Dickson, E. J. (2016). "Poldark writer Debbie Horsfield says Ross did not rape Elizabeth," *Radio Times*, http://www.radiotimes.com/news/2016-10-25/poldark-writer-debbie-horsfield-says-ross-did-not-rape-elizabeth (accessed 4 June 2018).

Dinos, Sokratis, et al. 2015. "A Systematic Review of Juries' Assessment of Rape Victims: Do Rape Myths Impact on Juror Decision-Making?" *International Journal of Law Crime and Justice*, vol. 43, pp. 36–49.

Donaghy, James. 2019. "The new and improved Das Boot – now with added women" *The Guardian*, https://www.theguardian.com/tv-and-radio/2019/feb/06/the-new-and-improved-das-boot-now-with-added-women (accessed 29 May 2021).

Doody, Margaret Anne. 1974. *A Natural Passion: A Study of the Novels of Samuel Richardson*. London: Clarendon Press.

Dowd-Arrow Emily, J. and Sarah R. Creel. 2016. "I Know You Want It": Teaching the Blurred Lines of Eighteenth-Century Rape Culture," *ABO: Interactive Journal for Women in the Arts, 1640–1830*, vol. 6:2, Article 2, https://digitalcommons.usf.edu/cgi/viewcontent.cgi?article=1110&context=abo (accessed 12 June 2021).

Downton Abbey (ITV, 2010–2015).

Doyle, Mika. 2019. "Male rape is no joke—But pop culture often treats it that way," *Bitch Media*, https://www.bitchmedia.org/article/male-rape-no-joke%E2%80%94-pop-culture-often-treats-it-way (accessed 1 June 2021).

The Duchess (Directed by Saul Dibb, 2008).

Ebert, Roger. 1980. "I spit on your grave" movie review, *RogerEbert.com*, https://www.rogerebert.com/reviews/i-spit-on-your-grave-1980 (accessed 5 May 2021).

Ellis, Lee. 1989. *Theories of Rape: Inquiries into the Causes of Sexual Aggression*. New York: Hemisphere Publishing.

Estrich, Susan. 1987. *Real Rape*. Cambridge, MA: Harvard University Press.

The Everyday Sexism Project, https://everydaysexism.com/.

Farhi, Paul. 2016. 'What is feminist hero Susan Estrich doing representing Roger Ailes?" *The Washington Post*, https://www.washingtonpost.com/lifestyle/style/feminist-hero-susan-estrich-fought-sexual-harassment-but-now-represents-roger-ailes-is-she-selling-out-or-standing-up/2016/08/04/904c22ce-5810-11e6-9aee-8075993d73a2_story.html (accessed 10 September 2021).

Farley, Melissa, et al. 2003. "Prostitution and trafficking in nine countries: An update on violence and posttraumatic stress disorder," *ResearchGate*, January 2003.

Ford, Clementine. 2016. "TV shows need to quit peddling the rape myth that 'no means yes'," *The Sydney Morning Herald*, https://www.smh.com.au/lifestyle/tv-shows-need-to-quit-peddling-the-rape-myth-that-no-means-yes-20161025-gs9r7f.html (accessed 5 May 2021).

The Forsyte Saga (BBC, 1967).

The Forsyte Saga (ITV, 2002).

The Frankenstein Chronicles (ITV Encore, 2015–2017).

Friday, Nancy. 1973: reprint 1996. *My Secret Garden: Women's Sexual Fantasies*. London: Quartet Books.

Friedman, Jonathan. 2002. *Speaking the Unspeakable: Essays on Sexuality, Gender, and the Holocaust Survivor Memory*. Lanham, MD: University Press of America.

Galsworthy, John. 2008 reprint. *The Forsyte Saga, Volume I: The Man of Property*. Oxford University Press.

Game of Thrones (HBO, 2011–2019).

Goh, Katie. 2018. "The Irish and Ulster rugby rape trial is not a one-off- this is what it's like to be a woman in Northern Ireland," *Independent*, https://www.independent.co.uk/voices/northern-ireland-ulster-rugby-rape-trial-not-guilty-im-with-her-a8280066.html (accessed 4 October 2018).

Goodman, Helen. 2012. "Madness in Marriage: Erotomania and Marital Rape in *He Knew He Was Right* and *The Forsyte Saga*," *Victorian Network*, 4:2 (Winter 2012), pp. 47–71.

Graham, Winston. 1953; repr. 2008. *Warleggan: A Novel of Cornwall, 1792-1793*. London: Pan Books.

Graham, Winston. 1973; reprint 1996. *The Black Moon: A Novel of Cornwall, 1794-1795*, London: Pan Books.

Graham, Winston. 1976; reprint 1996. *The Four Swans: A Novel of Cornwall, 1795-1797*, London: Pan Books.

Graham, Winston. 1984; reprint 2008. *The Loving Cup: A Novel of Cornwall, 1813-1815*, London: Pan Books.

Greer, Germaine. 2018. *On Rape*. London: Bloomsbury Publishing.

Grice, Elizabeth. "Shock is tempered as Soames strikes again," *The Telegraph*, 22 April 2002, http://www.telegraph.co.uk/news/uknews/1391733/Shock-is-tempered-as-Soames-strikes-again.html (accessed 5 June 2017).

Groskop, Vic. 2015. *Downton Abbey*: What should happen in the final episode? *The Guardian*, https://www.theguardian.com/tv-and-radio/tvandradioblog/2015/jan/29/downton-abbey-what-should-happen-in-the-final-episode (accessed 3 February 2021).

Gubar, Susan. 1987, "'This Is My Rifle, This Is My Gun': World War II and the Blitz on Women," in *Behind the Lines: Gender and the Two World Wars*, edited by M. Higonnet. Newhaven, CT: Yale University Press.

Gunter, Barrie, and Jackie Harrison. 1998. *Violence on Television: An Analysis of Amount, Nature, Location and Origin*. London: Routledge.

Halliday, Josh. 2013. "*Downton Abbey* rape scene defended by series creator Julian Fellowes," *The Guardian*, https://www.theguardian.com/tv-and-radio/2013/oct/08/downton-abbey-rape-scene-defended-julian-fellowes (accessed 10 April 2021).

Halliday, Josh. 2014 "Jimmy Savile: timeline of his sexual abuse and its uncovering," *Guardian*, 26 June. https://www.theguardian.com/media/2014/jun/26/jimmy-savile-sexual-abuse-timeline (accessed 25 May 2021).

Hannibal (NBC, 2013–2015).

Harlots (ITV Encore and Hulu, 2017–).

Harmon, Steph. 2019. *The Nightingale* director Jennifer Kent defends 'honest' depiction of rape and violence," *The Guardian*, 11 June, http://www.theguardian.com

/film/2019/jun/11/nightingale-director-jennifer-kent-defends-honest-depiction-of-and-violence (accessed 10 April 2021).

Harvey, Kerry. 2017. "A place to call Home's Sara Wiseman challenged by sexual assault storyline," *Stuff*, http://www.stuff.co.nz/entertainment/tv-radio/89893912/A-Place-To-Call-Homes-Sara-Wiseman-challenged-by-sexual-assault-storyline (accessed 10 April 2021).

Hedgepeth, Sonya, and Saidel, Rachel eds. 2010. *Sexual Violence against Jewish Women during the Holocaust*. Waltham, MA: Brandeis University Press.

Heim, Joe. 2014. "Downton Abbey' recap: An unthinkable act changes the tenor of the show," *The Washington Post*, https://www.washingtonpost.com/news/arts-and-entertainment/wp/2014/01/12/downton-abbey-recap-an-unthinkable-act-changes-the-tenor-of-the-show/ (accessed 10 April 2021).

Hitchcock, Tim. 1997. *English Sexualities: 1700-1800*. New York: St. Martin's Press.

Hollyoaks (Channel 4, 1995–).

Holmwood, Leigh. 2009. "Strictly ageism? Row as Arlene Phillips, 66, is axed for a 30-year-old," *The Guardian*, https://www.theguardian.com/media/2009/jul/17/arlene-phillips-strictly-come-dancing (accessed 4 June 2021).

Home Fires (ITV, 2015–2016).

Horeck, Tanya. 2004. *Public Rape: Representing Violation in Fiction and Film*. London: Routledge.

Hughes, Lauren. (2018). "Poldark star shares her reaction to fans' response to character's death," *what's on tv*, https://www.whatsontv.co.uk/news/poldark-star-reaction-fans-response-characters-death-548037/ (accessed 4 October 2018).

I May Destroy You (BBC and HBO, 2020).

Irish News. 2017. (https://www.irishnews.com/magazine/2017/01/24/news/emily-watson-hailed-for-immense-courage-filming-apple-tree-yard-rape-scene-903032/ (accessed 4 June 2021).

I Spit on Your Grave (Directed by Meir Zarchi, 1978).

Jamestown (Sky One, 2017–2019).

Javaid, Aliraza. 2016. "Feminism, masculinity and male rape: bringing male rape 'out of the closet,'" *Journal of Gender Studies*, vol. 25:3, pp. 283–293.

Jones, Paul. 2015. "Poldark's topless scything scene voted 2015 TV moment of the year," *Radio Times*, http://www.radiotimes.com/news/2015-12-31/poldarks-topless-scything-scene-voted-2015-tv-moment-of-the-year (accessed 3 June 2019).

Kellaway, Kate. 2013. "Helen McCrory: 'Most of the attention I get is from younger men,'" *The Guardian*, https://www.theguardian.com/culture/2013/apr/14/helen-mccrory-flying-blind-interview (accessed 5 June 2021).

Khomami, Nadia. (2017) "#MeToo: how a hashtag became a rallying cry against sexual harassment," *The Guardian*, https://www.theguardian.com/world/2017/oct/20/women-worldwide-use-hashtag-metoo-against-sexual-harassment (accessed 10 June 2021).

Krakauer, Steve. 2019. "Jeffrey Epstein's downfall and the crumbling of America's elites." *Think*, https://www.nbcnews.com/think/opinion/jeffrey-epstein-s-downfall-crumbling-america-s-elites-ncna1029966 (accessed 10 June 2021).

Ku' Damm 56 (Berlin Dance School) (UFA Fiction, 2016–2018).

Lamb, Christina. 2020. *Our Bodies, Their Battlefield: What War Does to Women*. Glasgow: William Collins.

Lazar, Ruthy Lowenstein. 2020. "Me Too? The Invisible Older Victims of Sexual Violence," *Michigan Journal of Gender and Law*, vol. 26:2, pp. 209–278.

Levy, Ariel. 2005. *Female Chauvinist Pigs: Women and the Rise of Raunch Culture*. New York: Free Press.

Linton, Phoebe C. 2015. "Modern Rape Culture and BBC's *Banished*," *Public Medievalist* (blog), http://www.publicmedievalist.com/modern-rape-culture-and-bbcs-banished/ (accessed 4 June 2018).

Loughrey, Clarisse. 2019. "Have horror movies made a monster out of the older woman?" *The Independent*, https://www.independent.co.uk/arts-entertainment/films/features/horror-movies-greta-isabelle-huppert-older-women-suspiria-what-ever-happened-baby-jane-a8878106.html (accessed 5 June 2021).

Lowen, Linda. 2013. "Using Downton Abbey Anna's rape to end the stigma of sexual violence," https://www.the-broad-side.com/using-downton-abbey-annas-rape-to-end-the-stigma-of-sexual-violence-linda-lowen (accessed 2 February 2021; article has since been removed).

Lyons, Margaret. 2014. "Yes, of course that was rape on last night's *Game of Thrones*," *Vulture*, https://www.vulture.com/2014/04/rape-game-of-thrones-cersei-jaime.html (accessed 10 September 2021).

Mad Men (AMC, 2007–2015).

Mahoney, Patricia and Williams, Linda M. 1998. "Sexual Assault in Marriage: Prevalence, Consequences, and Treatment of Wife Rape," *Semantic Scholar*, http://www.ncdsv.org/images/nnfr_partnerviolence_a20-yearliteraturereviewandsynthe-sis.pdf (accessed 6 May 2021).

Mandle, Chris. 2016. "Donald Trump's lawyer claims you can't rape your spouse after ivana trump historic "rape" allegations resurface'," http://www.independent.co.uk/ (accessed 20 May 20210).

Matthews, Nancy A. 1994. *Confronting Rape: The Feminist Anti-Rape Movement and the State*. New York: Routledge.

McHugh, Maureen C. and Camille Interligi. 2014. "Sexuality and Older Women: Desirability and Desire" in *Women and Aging: An International, Intersectional Power Perspective*, edited by Varda Muhlbauer, Joan C. Chrisler and Florence L. Denmark. New York: Springer.

McKee, David. 2016. Amazon review of *The Forsyte Saga* (1967), posted 7 January 2016, https://www.amazon.com/Forsyte-Saga-Complete-Eric-Porter/dp/B00007149J/ref=sr_1_fkmr0_1?ie=UTF8&qid=1496680624&sr=8-1-fkmr0&keywords=2005+dvd+forsyte+saga+1967 (accessed 5 May 2021).

McMillan, Graeme. 2014. "*Downton Abbey* and rape: Anna's excruciating Fridging problem," *Time*, https://time.com/9067/downtown-abbey-and-rape-anna-bates-fridging-problem/ (accessed 10 April 2021).

Mellor, Louisa. 2017. "*Poldark* series 3 episode 8 review" *Den of Geek*, 30 July 2017 https://www.denofgeek.com/tv/poldark-series-3-episode-8-review/ (accessed 20 May 2021).

Mills, Jennie.(2009. "Rape and the Construction of Female Sexuality in the Eighteenth Century," in *Sexual Perversions, 1670-1880*, edited by Julie Peakman. London: Palgrave.

Minister, Meredith. 2018. *Rape Culture on Campus*. Lanham, MD: Lexington Books.

Monk, Claire. 2011. *Heritage Film Audiences: Period Films and Contemporary Audiences in the UK*. Edinburgh: Edinburgh University Press.

Moore, Anna and Khan, Coco. 2019. "The fatal, hateful rise of choking during sex," *The Guardian*, https://www.theguardian.com/society/2019/jul/25/fatal-hateful-rise-of-choking-during-sex, (accessed 10 April 2021).

Moseley, Rachel and Goodman, Gemma. 2018. "Television Costume Drama and the Eroticised, Regionalised Body: *Poldark* and *Outlander*," in *Conflicting Masculinities: Men in Television Period Drama*, edited by Katherine Byrne, James Leggott, and Julie Anne Taddeo. London: I.B. Tauris, pp. 52–70.

Mrs. America (FX on Hulu, 2020).

Mumford, Gwilym. 2017. "Actor Terry Crews: I was sexually assaulted by Hollywood executive," *The Guardian*, https://www.theguardian.com/film/2017/oct/11/actor-terry-crews-sexually-assaulted-by-hollywood-executive (accessed 10 September 2021).

My Brilliant Friend (HBO, 2018–).

Napoli, Jessica. 2017. "Outlander' EPs on why they changed the controversial Jamie-Geneva sex scene," *TV Insider*, https://www.tvinsider.com/463901/outlander-executive-producers-change-jamie-geneva-sex-scene/ (accessed 1 June 2021).

Naugle, Wendy. 2019. "What *Outlander* finally gets right about rape this season," Glamour https://www.glamour.com/story/what-outlander-gets-right-about-rape-this-season (accessed 1 June 2021).

Navarro, Meagan. 2021. "'*Promising Young Woman*' and the Evolution of Rape-Revenge Films" *in Bloody Disgusting*, https://bloody-disgusting.com/editorials/3649032/promising-young-woman-departure-horror-rape-revenge-films-spoiler/ (accessed 10 April 2021).

Nguyen, Hanh. 2018. "*Harlots*' Review: Liv Tyler Joins the Cast for a Heartbreaking Season 2 Filled With Horrifying Machinations," *Indie Wire*, https://www.indiewire.com/2018/07/harlots-season-2-review-hulu-liv-tyler-1201984087/ (accessed 5 May 2021).

The Nightingale (Directed by Jennifer Kent, 2019).

O'Donovan, Gerard. 2016. "Poldark: in whose world is the Elizabeth-Ross rape scene consensual?" *The Telegraph*, http://www.telegraph.co.uk/tv/2016/10/23/poldark-in-whose-world-is-the-elizabeth-ross-rape-scene-consensu/ (Accessed 4 June 2018).

Olen, Helaine. 2019. "What the Jeffrey Epstein case says about American society," *The Lily*, https://www.thelily.com/what-the-jeffrey-epstein-case-says-about-american-society/? (accessed 5 May 2021).

Oliver, Sarah. 2018. "Tain't right, tain't proper – but look out Ross, Drake might just steal the show in... Poldark: Battle Of The Heart-Throbs," *Daily Mail*, https://www.dailymail.co.uk/home/event/article-5682783/Poldark-Battle-Heart-Throbs.html (accessed 6 June 2020).

Outlander (Starz, 2014–).
Palmer, Ewan. 2015. "David Cameron v Outlander: PM met with Sony execs to stop Scottish rebel drama before referendum vote," *International Business Times*, https://www.ibtimes.co.uk/david-cameron-v-outlander-pm-met-sony-execs-stop-scottish-rebel-drama-before-referendum-vote-1497534 (accessed 6 June 2021).
Peaky Blinders (BBC Two, 2013–).
Peterson, Latoya. 2009. "On *Mad Men*, When is it Rape?" *Jezebel*, https://jezebel.com/on-mad-men-when-is-it-rape-5374654, (accessed 4 June 2021).
Phillips, Nickie D. 2017. *Beyond Blurred Lines: Rape Culture in Popular Media*. Lanham, MD: Rowman & Littlefield.
Pickard, Michael. 2018. "Hot damm," *Drama Quarterly*, https://dramaquarterly.com/hot-damm/ (accessed 10 April 2021).
Poldark (BBC, 1975–1977).
Poldark (BBC, 2015–2019).
Power, Shannon, 2020. "GROUND BREAKING: I May Destroy You star insists Kwame's harrowing sexual assault is 'historic moment' for British TV," *The Sun*, https://www.thesun.co.uk/tvandshowbiz/12063475/i-may-destroy-you-kwame-sexual-assault-british/ (accessed 6 June 2021).
Prescott, Amanda. 2020. "How *Bridgerton* can avoid *Outlander*'s mistakes" *Den of Geek*, 10 December 2020, https://www.denofgeek.com/tv/how-bridgerton-can-avoid-outlanders-mistakes/ (accessed 5 May 2021).
Press, Joy. 2018. "Where did all the #MeToo TV shows go?" *Vanity Fair*, 4 October, https://www.vanityfair.com/hollywood/2018/10/the-impact-of-metoo-and-female-rage-on-tv-shows-and-hollywood (accessed 24 March 2019).
Projansky, Sarah. 2001. *Watching Rape: Film and Television in Postfeminist Culture*. New York: New York University Press.
Promising Young Woman (Directed by Emerald Fennell, 2020).
Prudom, Laura. 2013. "'Outlander' finale: Ron Moore on tackling rape scenes truthfully," *Variety*, https://variety.com/2015/tv/news/outlander-finale-season-2-spoilers-jamie-claire-1201508528/ (accessed 1 June 2021).
Quora. 2016. https://www.quora.com/Why-did-the-Game-of-Thrones-writers-have-Jaime-rape-Cersei-many-have-said-the-rape-scene-wasn%E2%80%99t-in-the-books-Why-include-this-scene-after-spending-so-much-time-making-Jaime-more-likable-And-why-did-Cersei-alienate-Jaime-when-he-first-came-back (accessed 15 September 2021).
Quinn, Julia. 2000. *The Duke and I*. New York: Avon Books (Kindle version).
Rabin, Nathan. 2007. "My year of flops, case file 1: Elizabethtown: The Bataan Death March of Whimsy," *The A.V. Club*. (accessed 5 January 2021).
Rackham, Annabel. 2018. "Coronation Street: The story behind David Platt's rape," *BBC News*, https://www.bbc.com/news/entertainment-arts-43473007, (accessed 1 June 2021).
Radio Times. 2016. https://www.radiotimes.com/news/2016-12-30/poldarks-topless-tin-bath-scene-voted-2016s-biggest-tv-moment/ (accessed 15 June 2018).
RAINN.org/statistics. 2020. https://www.rainn.org/statistics/victims-sexual-violence (accessed 3 June 2021).

Ramaswamy, Chitra. 2019. "Bodice-rippers! How period drama went from buttoned up to sexed up," *The Guardian*, December 28, 2019, https://www.theguardian.com/tv-and-radio/2019/dec/28/bodice-rippers-how-period-drama-went-from-buttoned-up-to-sexed-up (accessed 5 May 2021).

Ravitz, Jessica. 2011 "Silence lifted: The untold stories of rape during the Holocaust," *CNN* June 24, 2011—Updated 1123 GMT (1923 HKT), http://edition.cnn.com/2011/WORLD/europe/06/24/holocaust.rape/index.html (accessed 29 May 2021).

Read, Jacinda. 2002. *The New Avengers: Feminism, Femininity and the Rape-Revenge Cycle*. Manchester: Manchester University Press.

Reality Check Team (2014). "Queen bees: Do women hinder the progress of other women?" *BBC News*, 4th Jan. https://www.bbc.co.uk/news/uk-41165076 (accessed 5 May 2021).

The Restaurant (Sveriges Television, 2017–).

Richardson Niall. 2019. "Introduction: Identifying 'old' age – biological, cultural and social," in *Ageing Femininity on Screen: The Older Woman in Contemporary Cinema*, edited by N. Richardson. London and New York: I.B. Tauris, pp. 1–30.

Richardson, Valerie. 2020. "'Mrs. America,' Phyllis Schlafly miniseries, a feminist hit job, daughter Anne Schlafly Cori says," *Washington Times*, https://www.washingtontimes.com/news/2020/apr/14/mrs-america-phyllis-schlafly-miniseries-feminist-h/ (accessed 10 September 2021).

Rodger, James. 2019. "'Peaky Blinders' Helen McCrory reveals how Aunt Polly's brutal rape has helped real life victims," *Birmingham Mail*, https://www.birminghammail.co.uk/news/showbiz-tv/peaky-blinders-helen-mccrory-reveals-16848517 (accessed 4 June 2021).

Roiphe, Katie. 2012. "The sexual fantasies of the working woman," *The Star*, https://www.thestar.com/news/insight/2012/09/15/the_sexual_fantasies_of_the_working_woman.html (accessed 10 June 2021).

Romano, Aja. 2020. "*Bridgerton* has a rape scene, but it's not treated like one," *Vox*, https://www.vox.com/22194033/bridgerton-netflix-rape-scene-novel (accessed 1 June 2021).

Rubenhold, Hallie. 2005. *The Covent Garden Ladies*. Gloucestershire: Tempus.

Sarner, Lauren. 2017. "'Outlander' Gets Right What 'Game of Thrones' Got Wrong About Rape Consent on TV," *The Daily Beast*, https://www.thedailybeast.com/outlander-gets-right-what-game-of-thrones-got-wrong-about-rape-and-consent-on-tv (accessed 1 June 2021).

Schindler's List (Directed by Steven Spielberg, 1993).

Schultz, Randy. 2018. "Will Alex Acosta and other enablers face justice for Jeffrey Epstein?" *Florida Sun Sentinel*, https://www.sun-sentinel.com/opinion/fl-op-col-alex-acosta-20181204-story.html (accessed 24 March 2021).

Seltzer, Leon F. 2014. "Don't Call Them "Rape Fantasies!"" *Psychology Today*, https://www.psychologytoday.com/gb/blog/evolution-the-self/201411/don-t-call-them-rape-fantasies (accessed 10 October 2018).

Semigran, Rachel. 2013. "'Downton Abbey' Recap: We Need to Talk About Anna," *Bustle*, https://www.bustle.com/articles/12257-downton-abbey-recap-we-need-to-talk-about-annas-rape (accessed 10 April 2021).

Sexual Offences Act. 2003. https://www.legislation.gov.uk/ukpga/2003/42/contents (accessed 6 June 2021).

Sinnreich, Helene. 2008. "And it was something we didn't talk about: Rape of Jewish women during the Holocaust," *Holocaust Studies: A Journal of Culture and History*, vol. 14:2, pp. 1–22.

Sinnreich, Helene. 2010. "The Rape of Jewish Women during the Holocaust," in *Sexual Violence against Jewish Women During the Holocaust*, edited by Sonia Hedgepeth and Rachel Saidel. Waltham, MA: Brandeis University Press, pp. 108–123.

The Sopranos (HBO, 1999–2007).

The Stern Review. 2010. *A report by Baroness Vivien Stern CBE of an Independent Review into How Rape Complaints are Handled by Public Authorities in England and Wales*. Government Equalities Office: Home Office.

The Straight Dope Message Board. 2017. http://boards.straightdope.com/sdmb/showthread.php?t=238836 (accessed 5 May 2021).

Taboo (BBC One, 2017–).

Taddeo, Julie Anne. 2014. "'Why Don't You Take Her?': Rape in the *Poldark* Narrative," in *Upstairs and Downstairs: British Costume Drama Television from The Forsyte Saga to Downton Abbey*, edited by James Leggott and Julie Anne Taddeo. Lanham, MD: Rowman and Littlefield, pp. 207–221.

Taddeo, Julie Anne. 2018. "The war is done. Shut the door on it!": The Great War, Masculinity and Trauma in British Period Television," in *Conflicting Masculinities: Men in Television Period Drama*, edited by Katherine Byrne, James Leggott, and Julie Anne Taddeo. London: I.B. Tauris, pp. 165–186.

Taddeo, Julie Anne. 2019. "Let's talk about sex: Period Drama Histories for the Twenty-first Century," *Journal of British Cinema and Television*, vol. 16:1, pp. 42–60.

Taylor, Frances. 2017. "Was Banished cancelled after one series because of Poldark?" *Radio Times*, https://www.radiotimes.com/news/2017-07-31/was-banished-cancelled-after-one-series-because-of-poldark/ (accessed 4 October 2018).

Taylor, Jessica. 2016. "Feminist Tropes: Corsetry and Rape in Saul Dibb's *The Duchess*," *Journal of Media & Cultural Studies*, vol. 30:3, pp. 336–346.

Teo, Hsu-Ming. 1996. "The Continuum of Sexual Violence in Occupied Germany, 1945-49," *Women's History Review*, 5:2, pp. 191–218.

Topping, Alexandra. 2018. "Quarter of adults think marital sex without consent is not rape, UK survey finds," *The Guardian*, https://www.theguardian.com/society/2018/dec/06/quarter-of-adults-think-marital-sex-without-consent-is-not-uk-survey-finds (accessed 5 May 2021)

Tovey, Josephine. 2015. "Game of Thrones: Fans 'quit' show after controversial Sansa Stark rape scene," *The Sydney Morning Herald*, https://www.smh.com.au/entertainment/tv-and-radio/game-of-thrones-fans-quit-show-after-controversial-sansa-stark-rape-scene-20150519-gh4ldi.html (accessed 4 June 2021).

Tripodi, Francesca. 2017. "Fifty shades of consent?" *Feminist Media Studies*, vol. 17:1, pp. 93–107.

Tu, Jessie. 2020. "1 in 3 young men don't consider punching a form of domestic abuse, according to new, White Ribbon research," https://womensagenda.com

.au/latest/1-in-3-young-men-dont-consider-punching-a-form-of-domestic-abuse-according-to-new-white-ribbon-research/ (accessed 24 May 2021).

Valby, Karen. 2014. "Hey TV: Stop raping women," *Entertainment Weekly*, https://ew.com/article/2014/02/27/tv-rape-scenes-downton-abbey-house-of-cards-scandal/ (accessed 11 June 2021).

Van Arendonk, Kathryn. 2018. "*Outlander* drew a line between rape and sex. Does it need so much rape, Though?" *Vulture*, https://www.vulture.com/2018/12/outlander-season-4-sex-rape-wilmington.html (accessed 24 March 2019).

Vanstone, Ellen. 2016. "How has rape become such a common trope of television drama?" https://www.theglobeandmail.com/arts/television/how-has-rape-become-such-a-common-trope-of-television-drama/article31931181/ (accessed 11June 2021).

Velvet Colección (Bambu Producciones, 2017–2019).

Vineyard, Jennifer. 2020. "How the 'Outlander' Team Managed That Shocking Season Finale," *The New York Times*, https://www.nytimes.com/2020/05/10/arts/television/outlander-finale-caitriona-balfe-diana-gabaldon.html (accessed 4 June 2021).

Walkowitz, Judith. 1992. *City of Dreadful Delight: Narratives of Sexual Danger in Late-Victorian London*. Chicago: University of Chicago Press.

Ward, James. 2018. "The Masculine Economies of *Banished*," in *Conflicting Masculinities: Masculinity in British Period Drama Television*, edited by Katherine Byrne, James Leggott, and Julie Anne Taddeo. London: I.B. Tauris, pp. 15–34.

Watt, Ian. 1971. *The Rise of the Novel: Studies in Defoe, Richardson and Fielding*. Berkeley: University of California Press.

The Week. 2018. "When did marital rape become a crime? 'Alarming' new statistics show that a quarter of Brits do not view non-consensual sex within marriage as rape," https://www.theweek.co.uk/98330/when-did-marital-rape-become-a-crime (accessed 5 May 2021).

Weekes, Princess. 2018. "Because of time's up and me too, *Outlander* may finally have to deal with its rape problem next season," *The Mary Sue*, https://www.themarysue.com/timesup-metoo-outlander-rape-problem/ (accessed 10 April 2021).

Weiss, Norman. 2018. "*Outlander* will be extra sensitive about depicting sexual assault in wake of the #MeToo era," *PrimeTimer*, https://www.primetimer.com/item/Outlander-will-be-extra-sensitive-about-depicting-sexual-assault-In-wake-of-the-MeToo-era-YESB9N (accessed 10 April 2021).

Whelehan Imelda. 2013. "Ageing Appropriately: Postfeminist Discourses of Ageing in Contemporary Hollywood," in *Postfeminism and Contemporary Hollywood Cinema*, edited by Joel Gwynne and Muller Nadine. London: Palgrave Macmillan, pp. 78–95.

Willsher, Kim. 2020. "France detains modelling agent in Jeffrey Epstein inquiry," *The Guardian*, https://www.theguardian.com/world/2020/dec/17/france-detains-modelling-agent-jean-luc-brunel-in-jeffrey-epstein-inquiry (accessed 5 May 2021).

Wilson, Anna. 2001. *Persuasive Fictions: Feminist Narrative and Critical Myth*. Lewisburg, PA: Bucknell University Press.

Wilson, Benjy. 2015. "Lust, brutality and the birth of Oz: Floggings, rape and hangings, a harrowing new drama follows the first British convicts deported to Australia," *Daily Mail*, https://www.dailymail.co.uk/femail/article-2958609/Lust-brutality-birth-Oz-Floggings-rape-hangings-harrowing-new-drama-follows-British-convicts-deported-Australia.html (accessed 24 March 2019).

Wolf, Naomi. 1991. *The Beauty Myth: How Images of Beauty Are Used Against Women*. New York: Doubleday.

World on Fire (BBC One, 2019–).

Wyatt, Daisy. 2013. "Downton Abbey creator Julian Fellowes defends rape scene: "We're interested in exploring the emotional damage," *The Independent*, https://www.independent.co.uk/arts-entertainment/tv/news/downton-abbey-creator-julian-fellowes-defends-rape-scene-we-re-interested-exploring-emotional-damage-8868427.html (accessed 10 April 2021).

YouTube Fan Comments. (2017). https://www.youtube.com/watch?v=F9f0J1W0Dys (accessed 25/03/2019).

YouTube Fan Comments. (2019). https://www.youtube.com/watch?v=CHWqevc2ZH8 (assessed 25 March 2019).

Index

Accused, The, 53
age of consent, 78
anti-Semitism, 33
Apple Tree Yard, 110–12

Banished, 7–21, 29, 31, 36, 48, 53, 57, 70, 71
Batman Returns, 36
Berlin Dance School, 33–36
Bletchley Circle, 71
Bridgerton, 3, 5, 43, 45–57, 93, 124
Brownmiller, Susan, 43, 60, 65, 69, 75, 99, 104, 114
Butterflies, 16

campus Rape, 33–37. *See also* *Promising Young Woman*
choking during sex, 34
Clarissa. *See* Richardson, Samuel
coercion, 12–14, 48, 54
complicit society and rape, 2, 24, 33, 37, 38, 53, 65, 66, 80, 95, 100, 115
consent, 4, 7, 9–13, 26, 34, 35, 45–47, 50, 82, 86, 91–93, 98, 99, 103, 104
Coronation Street, 44–45
COVID-19, 124

Das Boot, 4, 59–75

Downton Abbey, 2, 3, 19, 25–28, 31, 39, 40, 54, 59, 81, 113, 124
Duchess, The, 19, 93–94, 100

eighteenth-century rape culture, 81–89
Epstein, Jeffrey, 2, 38, 77–79, 85, 87–89

Fifty Shades of Grey, 17
Forsyte Saga, The, 93–99, 104–5
Frankenstein Chronicles, The, 89
Friday, Nancy (*My Secret Garden*), 16, 18
"fridging," 30

Gabaldon, Diana, 37, 48, 113. *See also* *Outlander*
Game of Thrones, 17, 108
gang rape, 53, 64, 113, 115
Gothic fiction, 15
Hammer Horror (film company), 15, 49
harassment in the workplace, 26, 28, 31, 32, 112, 119
Harlots, 4–5, 77–89
heritage film, 1, 18, 113
Hollyoaks, 44, 45

I May Destroy You, 45
I Spit on Your Grave, 23, 107

Index

Jamestown, 1

Ku'damm, 56. See also Berlin Dance School

Mad Men, 33, 111–12
male rape, 3, 43–57, 109, 124; by women, 45–51
marital rape, 2, 5, 14, 19, 70, 91–106, 109, 111, 114
Maxwell, Ghislaine, 79–80
menopause, 108, 113, 115
mental health, 18
#MeToo, 1–7, 16, 21, 24–26, 36–38, 45–56, 60, 65, 66, 80–81, 100, 103, 109, 111, 113, 115, 118, 124
middle-aged women, 6, 24, 49, 102, 109–20
Mrs America, 104
My Brilliant Friend, 92, 109

Nazism, 33, 62
Nightingale, The, 24
"no means yes," 9, 13, 19
nostalgia, 1, 5, 94, 124

Outlander, 5, 6, 15, 25, 26, 37–41, 47–57, 65, 70, 92, 100, 107, 112–17, 124

Peaky Blinders, 6, 113, 117–21
penetration, importance of in law, 47
Phineas Finn, 92
A Place to Call Home, 25, 31–33, 59–74, 103
Poldark, 2, 3, 5, 7–21, 29, 31, 36, 48, 52, 53, 57, 91–125
pornography, 10, 18, 19, 34, 53, 102, 109

"positive outcome rape scenes," 10
pregnancy, 12, 39, 46, 49, 72, 102
Promising Young Woman, 23, 24, 35, 40
PTSD in rape survivors, 82, 103; in war, 70, 72

Radio Times, 8, 104
RAINN, 28, 44, 107
rape fantasy, 7, 9, 14–21
rape in war, 61–75
rape law, 11, 24, 35, 40, 47, 78, 82, 88, 91–92, 95, 97, 99, 103–6, 119, 124
rape-revenge, 23, 30, 36, 39, 107, 110
"raunch culture," 97
"ravishment," 2–3, 7, 16, 18, 20, 49. See also "no means yes"
Richardson, Samuel, 15
romance plots, 3, 6, 16, 18, 36, 39, 46, 57, 94, 102, 103, 105
Rosemary's Baby, 15

sex work, 77, 79–83. See also Harlots
"slash" fan fiction, 53
Sopranos, The, 110
Stead, W. T., 78
Stern Review, 47
stranger rape, 2, 11, 26, 91, 92, 100, 107, 110, 124

#TimesUp, 1, 124

Velvet Colección, 49
vigilante (victim becoming), 36

Weinstein, Harvey, 2, 31, 38, 89
witches, 3, 49, 114
World War 2. See rape in war

About the Authors

Dr. Katherine Byrne teaches English at Ulster University, United Kingdom. She is the author of *Tuberculosis and the Victorian Literary Imagination* (2011) and *Edwardians on Screen: From Downton Abbey to Parade's End* (2015), and is one of the editors of *Conflicting Masculinities: Men in Television Period Drama* (2018). Her research interests include Victorian literature and medicine, adaptation and period drama, women's writing, and Gothic studies, and she has published widely in all these areas.

Dr. Julie Anne Taddeo is research professor of history at University of Maryland, the United States. She is the author of *Lytton Strachey and the Search for Modern Sexual Identity* (2002), the editor of *Catherine Cookson Country: On the Borders of Legitimacy, Fiction, and History* (2012), and a coeditor of *Conflicting Masculinities: Men in Television Period Drama* (2018) and *Upstairs and Downstairs: British Costume Drama Television from* The Forsyte Saga *to* Downton Abbey (2015). Her research and teaching interests include Victorian sexuality, the history of masculinity, and British period drama television.

www.ingramcontent.com/pod-product-compliance
Lightning Source LLC
Chambersburg PA
CBHW061718300426
44115CB00014B/2737